The ^IM Perfect Storm
From HENRY STREET To HOLLYWOOD

**By Howard Storm
& Steve Stoliar**

Introduction by Dick Cavett

Published in the USA by:

BearManor Media
4700 Millenia Blvd.
Suite 175 PMB 90497
Orlando, FL 32839
www.bearmanormedia.com

Paperback ISBN: 978-1-62933-496-7
Case ISBN: 978-1-62933-497-4
Printed in the United States of America
Book design by Robbie Adkins, www.adkinsconsult.com
Cover design by Steve Stoliar

*This book is dedicated to
my parents – Jack and Anne Sobel.*

INTRODUCTION

Many and many a year ago, Howard Storm and I worked end-lessly it seemed, night after night, in a dinky Greenwich Village nightclub, "Upstairs at the Duplex." No pay, but a place to work and shape your act. Nobody had heard of either of us. I always watched Howard do his act, admiring his crisp style and his onstage confi-dence. Or (just as good) his ability to simulate it.

Surely a tough New York Lower East Side childhood contrib-uted to how he fearlessly faced those not always "wonderful folks out front." Especially the Neanderthals among them who decide, after copious firewater, that they too are comedy "artistes" with witticisms worth shouting out to enhance the evening's fun. That detested breed, the "heckler." I never saw Howard fail to bury them. It would sound like:

Howard: "Sir, what you are doing is heckling me. The dictionary defines 'heckling' as 'baiting,' and as far as baiting is concerned, you are a master."

Mr. Storm is shorter than I am, bless his heart, but he always seemed to out-measure me when onstage.

Toughening by that childhood on the storied Lower East Side – with its gangs of tough guys, real gangsters, violent stickball, fist-fights, robberies, and dwellings the opposite of luxury – all helped to produce a man who, despite limited stature, could, as the saying goes, take care of himself. Onstage and off. As for the inevitable fistfights, he appears to have survived them without – as S.J. Perel-man brilliantly put it – having his salients rearranged.

Time passed and acting jobs in television and films came and led to more of them, enough to satisfy most showbiz aspirants. But note the almost magic way Howard's thespian life dissolves gradu-ally into the exalted rank of television _director_, a job which Howard quickly demonstrates a marked talent for as his career moves up from "making the rounds" to being one of television's most sought –

and most employed – directors. The kid from the Lower East Side is soon handling, shepherding, calming and firmly correcting the biggest stars on the biggest shows.

Howard's adventures in the world of directing take you inside a colorful, painful, thrilling, combative, shocking, adventurous world of talent, ego, some artistry, headaches, nerves, unexpected triumphs, and, yes, famous people being pains-in-the-arse.

(They seem so nice on the screen.)

Have I mentioned that Howard is a born storyteller? It's often a case of, "Here comes Howard. Great! Here comes a story." I was in a play Howard directed and he'd come around before curtain time and regale the cast. His is a God-given gift, with perfect diction, faultless foreign dialects and perfect pacing and timing and "right word" selection, each story a kind of master class in tale-telling and always building to a powerful punchline and laugh. The cast loved these story visits to our crowded group dressing room. (I noticed Howard's actorly instinct always took him to the currently best-lighted part of the room.)

As an act of public service, Howard and writer Steve Stoliar – author of the popular book *Raised Eyebrows* about life inside Groucho's house – have compiled this wonderfully entertaining collection of tales, exactly as Howard speaks them. I guess you'd call his style "present tense narrative." As in: "So I walk into the room, I take off my hat," etc. Stoliar's shrewd shaping of the material keeps pulling you along no matter what else you thought you'd be doing today.

Show business is a series of doors. But how to get through them? Howard Storm is one who would not be beaten by the cruel odds, spending the rest of his life lamenting that he "just didn't get the breaks." He refused to crumple. He managed to get through those daunting portals. Most do not.

He manages to look back on it all with a healthy satisfaction. And why not? This is a terrific book about a man who has survived a tough life while seeming somehow to have enjoyed almost all of it. A man who beat the odds, endured the batterings, and can say with conviction, "I am a happy man." What an enviable minority to be in.

Enjoy the book and see for yourself why we Howard Storm admirers like him so: for his intelligence, talents, guts, generosity and kindness. To put it simply, we have great affection for Howard. So will you.

– Dick Cavett
May 2018

ACKNOWLEDGEMENTS

First off, I would like to thank my co-author, Steve Stoliar, who shaped this book so beautifully. Special thanks to Dick Cavett for his wonderful introduction. Thanks also go out to those who graciously contributed to the creation of this book: Woody Allen, Mel Brooks, Billy Crystal, Pam Dawber, Alix & Budd Friedman, Richard Lewis, Bob Newhart, and Rick Sandack (who gave me the title).

I would also like to thank friends and colleagues – some still here; some no longer with us – who helped me throughout my career and personal life: Lou Alexander, Dr. Paul Bradlow, Allan Burns, Tony Cacciotti, Dave Davis, Karen & Victor Earle, Billy Fields, Valerie Harper, Charlie Joffe, Garry Marshall, Frank Pace, Jack Rollins, and especially my sons – Anthony and Casey – who make me proud every day.

Finally, my thanks and love – not necessarily in that order – to my wife, Patricia, who edited this book and who stood beside me, cheering me on, every step of the way.

PROLOGUE

It's the mid-1950s. I'm a struggling young comic willing to play any club that'll pay me, even if it's run by the mob, which most of them are. There's a club in Youngstown, Ohio called The Copa that's owned by a mob guy named Shaky Naples, part of a notorious crime family out of Pittsburgh. Shaky has a bodyguard named Big Ralph. Next to the club is a lounge, also owned by Shaky. One night, I walk into the lounge and Big Ralph says, "Hey kid, have a drink." I tell him, "Thanks, I don't drink." He pulls out a gun and repeats, "I said have a *drink!*" This time, I say, "I'll have a bottle of scotch!" Everybody in the bar laughs and it becomes a ritual: Every time I walk in, Big Ralph pulls a gun on me.

As you might imagine, the joke wears thin pretty fast. The third time Big Ralph pulls out his gun, I tell him, "Do me a favor. Stick that gun up your ass." He says, "Oh, you're not afraid of dying?" I tell him, "It's not dying I'm afraid of, it's *waiting* to die. I don't know what it's like to die, so I'm not afraid of that, but what I am afraid of is you pointing a gun at me. So if you're gonna point it, either shoot me or I'm walking away." I start to leave and I'm thinking, "I'm gonna get shot in the back." But I walk away – unharmed.

Back at The Copa, I'm in my dressing room. Big Ralph comes in with Shaky's kid brother, Billy. They pull out their guns and Big Ralph says, "Give us all your money." I tell him, "I got twenty dollars. If *that's* gonna save me from getting shot, here." Big Ralph says, "That ain't enough. Come with us." They walk me down the hall into Shaky's office and sit me down. Big Ralph opens a desk drawer. There's a pistol inside. He asks me, "Do you know what that is?" I pick it up and I say, "Yeah, it's a .38 special." They put their guns away. Big Ralph says, "Do you know how to use it?" I tell him, "I'm not sure. I think I squeeze the trigger and the bullet comes out here and hits you in the chest." Now I see the blood starting to drain from their faces. Billy turns to open the door.

Suddenly, I go nuts. I become Jimmy Cagney. I tell Billy, "Don't touch the door or I'll put a bullet in your ass! Turn around!" Even as this is happening, I realize the situation is out of control. I tell them, "Both of you, hands on your heads!" They're standing with their hands on their heads, these two tough guys. I'm thinking, "I got two guys who have guns, but they haven't got 'em out and I'm standing here holding a .38 special on 'em. What's the next move?"

And how the hell did I get myself into this situation?

CHAPTER ONE

My name is Howard Storm. I'm an actor, standup comic and director. I was born on December 11, 1931, on the kitchen floor at 252 Madison Street on New York's Lower East Side. In those days, during the Depression, they give you an apartment one month free, so everybody moves in for a month and then moves to another apartment. After moving three or four times, our family settles on 172 Henry Street. It's a five-room railroad flat with no doors, so you can see all the way down the hallway. The only sink is in the kitchen; the bathroom doesn't have one.

On the day I am to be born, my mother sends for the doctor. When he shows up, she tells him, "I'm ready!" He tells her, "No you're not." She says, "Doctor, this is the third child I've had and I *know* when I'm ready." He says, "I'm the doctor and you're not ready." He slams the door and leaves. Twenty minutes later, her water breaks. I'm delivered by a neighbor's son, who's studying to be a doctor. In my standup act, I say, "I was delivered by a neighbor's son – a plumber. My father said he knew I was born on the kitchen floor, because he heard the water running."

My father's birth name is Zayde Sloboda. My grandmother in Bialystok, Russia, had two healthy daughters, but one son died before he was a year old and the other one was stillborn. So when my father is born, the rabbi says, "If you want this boy to live a long life, name him Zayde," which means "grandpa" in Yiddish. It works: He lives to be ninety-one. My father – "Grandpa" Sloboda – is four years old when he comes to America in either 1900 or 1902, along with his mother and two older sisters. He speaks Russian but mostly Yiddish. All the Yiddish kids at school know that "Zayde" means "Grandfather" and they tease him, so he changes his name to the all-American "Jack."

In those days, everybody leaves school in the 8th grade to help their family. In either 1912 or 1914, my father is called into the office of the principal, who tells him, "You're too dumb to be anything but an actor, so I've set up an audition for you with a friend of mine named Gus Edwards." Gus Edwards is a *major* producer in vaudeville. He produces an act called *School Days* with The Crazy Kids who, at that time, include Eddie Cantor, Georgie Jessel, Fanny Brice and Groucho Marx, among others. Walter Winchell – then a tap dancer – is part of the group, as is Bert Gordon, who later plays The Mad Russian on *The Eddie Cantor Show*. My father auditions and gets the job. He's in the second company, playing what they call "The Jew Comic." At the time, it isn't considered rude to say "Jew Comic" or "Wop Comic" or "Mick Comic."

My father is with Gus Edwards for quite a while and he manages to save two hundred dollars, which is *major* in those days. He decides to give his parents half of the money – a hundred dollars. He walks in, puts the hundred dollars down, and my grandfather slaps it off the table, saying, "Nobody but *gangsters* makes that kind of money!" My grandfather figures his son must be a gangster, because my father grew up with those guys. The neighbors are Louis "Lepke" Buchalter, Nathan "Kid Dropper" Kaplan, Jacob "Gurrah" Shapiro and Meyer Lansky! These are his contemporaries. They're tough. *Very* tough. When they're about fourteen, they stand on the corner with Kid Dropper, who takes bets that he can knock a horse down. He walks up and bang! He punches a horse and down it goes.

One Yom Kippur day, my father and Kid Dropper are standing on a corner with a guy who is a light-heavyweight amateur fighter. Four Irish guys in a horse and buggy come by. Some elderly Orthodox Jews are walking to the river to atone for their sins and the four Irish guys jump off the horse and buggy and start pulling the Jews' *payos* and taking their hats. My father and his friends turn the wagon over, break out the thick wooden spokes, and use them to beat the hell out of the Irish bullies! As I say, these are really tough guys.

Years later, when my father is working as a vaudeville comic at the Loew's Delancey, Kid Dropper comes backstage to see him, along with Jacob "Little Augie" Orgen, who carries a potato peeler with him as his weapon of choice. They come to say hello to my father, but in the alleyway of the theatre, they get into a fight and Augie cuts Dropper with his potato peeler. My father also cut Dropper, but he doesn't mean to. In the winter, when they're kids, they don't have sleds, so they take the tops off of five-gallon milk cans and go up on a hill in the snow. One kid sits in it and they push him, so he goes sliding down the hill. My father is pushing Dropper and he decides to jump on Dropper's shoulders to get an extra ride, but it forces their weight down on the metal milk-can cover and Dropper gets a big cut around his ass. After that, whenever Dropper sees my father, he tells him, "You're the only guy who ever scarred me – and got away with it!" He calls him "Slobbo" because of "Sloboda." That becomes my father's nickname to all the guys.

Another tough kid in my father's neighborhood is Jacob "Gurrah" Shapiro, a little fat kid who comes over to the States after the others are already here. In the winter, my father and his pals change the tracks for the trolley cars so the driver doesn't have to hop off into the snow. They switch it and the driver throws them a penny or two. One day, this kid comes yelling, "Gurrah from here! Gurrah!!" With his thick Yiddish accent, that's how "Get outta here!" comes out, so his nickname becomes Gurrah. Even at five or six, he's chasing the other kids away. They laugh at him, but years later, Gurrah Shapiro becomes Louis Lepke's right-hand man and they form Murder Incorporated!

During the Depression, my father sells ties. He goes to see Lepke. Gurrah greets him in the outer office and Lepke tells him to come in. He asks, "What's goin' on, Slobbo?" My father says, "I'm selling these ties and I wondered if you wanted to buy one or two." Lepke asks, "How many do you have?" My father says, "Twenty." He asks, "How much are they?" My father says, "A dollar each." Lepke tells him, "Okay, I'll take all twenty," and he peels off a twenty-dollar bill and gives it to him. At that time, a twenty-dollar bill is like a thou.

That's a nice story. Everybody has a "nice" story about those guys, but they're killers: literally "bad guys." All the guys in my father's neighborhood are tough guys. They *have* to be. Either that or they get beat up. Some of them become professional fighters, some become gangsters. Even my father is a tough guy. One day, he turns a corner and sees my brother, Eddie, surrounded by four guys. A woman is coming out of the store with a bag of groceries and a big Pepsi-Cola, so my father grabs the bottle of Pepsi, walks into the middle of the group and says, "Anybody touches him and I'll fracture your skulls!" Sure enough, the waters part. Twice, my brother watches him knock a guy out in the street with one punch.

My father can really box and he loves it. As a hobby, he gets a license to be a cut man. Because he works with different boxers, my brother and I get to see fights in every arena in New York: St. Nicholas Arena in midtown Manhattan, the Ridgewood Grove in Brooklyn, Sunnyside Gardens in Queens. We always get to sit ringside. I see Bummy Davis fight. He's from Brownsville, New York and he's the big hero. Bummy is a Jewish kid with blond, wavy hair, who has a great left hook and is a great fighter. We see a couple of neighborhood fighters in the ring. One is Maxie Shapiro, who's a terrific boxer. He fights Sugar Ray Robinson and Robinson knocks him out cold. Other great local fighters are Herbie Kronowitz, Harold Green and Danny Kopolow, who goes back to college after the war and becomes the administrator of a hospital in the Bronx.

CHAPTER TWO

Eventually, my father outgrows Gus Edwards and teams up with a guy named Benny Ross, a Jewish kid from Boston who's tough as nails. He's also a pool hustler. My father says they make more money hustling pool than they do with their act. Whenever they're out of town, they go to a pool hall. Benny hustles and my father is his shill.

There's a period in Boston when they have something called the Sunday Blue Laws, where there's no drinking and no act with music can work. Because of the Blue Laws, acts that don't need music pick up Sunday dates. My father and Benny Ross get an offer for a job in Boston. They get to the hall and there are two white tap dancers on the bill. My father asks, "What are you guys doin' here? You need music." One of them says, "We put something together." The dance team goes out first – and they do my father and Benny Ross' act verbatim! Benny and my father are standing backstage watching this and they can't believe it. As the two guys come offstage, Benny slugs both of them: Bang! Bang! He knocks them both down, turns to my father and says, "C'mon, Jack, take a bow; it's *our* act!" They go out, take a bow, collect the money and leave.

My father is never very successful as an entertainer. He struggles in vaudeville during the Depression and then, when vaudeville runs its course, he gets into burlesque. He hates La Guardia, because the mayor feels that burlesque is tacky, so he bans it in New York. It's silly, because people still want to see burlesque, so they just go across the river to Jersey.

When my father is dating my mother, Anne, he sings songs to try to win her over. One day, he tells her to meet him at City Hall and bring money. He brings a friend named Abe Kalish – who later becomes double-talk comedian Al Kelly – to be a witness at the wedding. Early in his career, my father uses the names Jack Stanton and Jack Stanley, but when he marries my mother in 1924, he changes the family name from Sloboda to Sobel and he is Jack Sobel for the rest of his life.

My sister Sylvia is their first child. My brother Eddie comes several years later. I'm the baby in the family. I'm named after my father's mother, Harriet, whom my father just adored. He really was spoiled silly. His mother doted on him and three sisters adored him and took care of him. He marries my mother and when he isn't working, he does nothing, although he still gets all dressed up every day, as if he has somewhere to go.

On my third birthday, my father presents me with a poem he's written, which a friend of his − in prison − has hand-lettered because he is so skilled in calligraphy. It is entitled *"Howard,"* is dated *"December 11, 1934,"* and is as follows:

"The first time you saw daylight
Was three years ago to-day
When you came to Dad and Mother
Now we hope and pray you'll stay.
You're a talkative little fellow
But we love you just the same
They should have called you Phonograph
But you got my Mother's name.
May her soul in peace be rested
Her habits were sublime.
She sure would love to hear you say
'Come up and see me sometime.'
They needed an Angel in Heaven
So they took my Mother Dear
And you came down to take her place
To bring us joy and cheer.
If her soul into your body
Was injected then it's true
Just like your Mother and Dad
The whole world will Love You too.
− Dad"

More than eighty years later, it remains a remarkable work and a treasured memento of my father.

In those days, no one has a phone, so people depend on the phone in the neighborhood candy store. On the weekend, my friends and I fight over getting to the phone, because guys are calling their dates. We hang out in the candy store, the phone rings, we grab it, and this is how it goes: "Who is this?" "This is Howie. I live on 172 Henry." "Okay, listen kid, do me a favor. This is Charlie. Go over to 164 Henry and tell Judy Schwartz that Charlie's gonna be a half-hour late." I say, "How much will you give me?" He says, "A nickel." I say, "No, I want a dime." He says, "Okay, a dime." Then I go stand in the street and yell up to the window. A woman comes to the window, "What is it?" "Charlie called." "What did he say?" "First, throw me down the dime." She wraps a dime in a piece of newspaper and throws it down and then I yell, "He's gonna be a half-hour late." She says, "You little *gonif!*" because she feels like I hustled her for the dime.

When my father's on the road with burlesque people who like to gamble and drink, he's very strait-laced. He takes a job for two weeks, but the morning after he gets there, he calls the candy store and they send someone to get my mother. He tells her, "If you're not out here by tomorrow morning, I'm quitting," because he doesn't want to be alone. I'm about eight, Eddie is thirteen and Sylvia is sixteen and a half. She's a young woman and a wonderful cook – better than my mother. They become my surrogate parents and we're happy whenever our mother goes on the road to join my father.

We come home from school and there, in the middle of the kitchen table, is Silver Cup Bread standing straight up – a whole loaf. In between every two slices of bread is bologna, and that's lunch for the week. There's a note that says, "I'm with Dad in Ohio." As soon as we open the door, whoever sees the bread first yells, "Mom's gone!" We don't feel abandoned. We're fine being left to fend for ourselves. I go to school. My sister cooks and makes dinner for us. I can always get lunch in school: Peanut butter sandwich with a bruised apple. Also, in those days, you're taken care of by your neighbors. Everybody watches out for everybody else.

Some nights when my mother's home, she leans over her side of the bed and calls down to my brother and me in the back bedroom:

"Anybody in the mood for pizza?" My brother and I jump up and yell, "Yeah!" and off we go. In those days, they don't sell pizza by the slice – it's always a whole pie – and they don't have white boxes to put them in. They use cardboard from a carton, and they put the pizza on the cardboard and put it in a bag. So in the winter, I walk home with the pizza and my feet are freezing from the slush and the cold, but my hand is burning from the grease dripping down from the hot pizza.

I go to see my dad in a burlesque theatre and Alan Alda's father, Robert Alda – real name "Alphonso D'Abruzzo" – is the juvenile for my father. He's a young guy and he sings "A Pretty Girl is Like A Melody." I go on matinees and hang out backstage. I sit in the box seats and my father introduces me and has me take a bow. I realize that the box seat is too high for them to see me, so I stand on the chair and bow. The strippers make a big a fuss over me backstage. Every Friday night, the cast comes to our apartment. My mother makes a big dinner and it's great fun. They tell jokes and are just a terrific bunch of lively, loving people. When I'm about eight or nine, the girls make me a G-string and pasties and I do a strip-tease dance. I love it. It gives me a chance to entertain, to perform, and I'm a ham. A kosher ham.

When I'm about nine, my father becomes the social director of a hotel in the Catskills. Once in a while, he brings me out onstage. We do stuff like, "How old are you?" "Nine." "Are you married?" Jokes that have been done a hundred times. He teaches me timing by holding my sleeve. He tells a joke and when the laughs subside, he lets go of my sleeve and I set up the next joke for him. As soon as he gets the laugh, he holds my sleeve again. Timing is very important, because if you hold too long, it's not good, but if you go too soon, it's not good either. One day, my father tells me, "Tonight you're on your own. I'm not gonna hold your sleeve." I'm very nervous. The laugh comes and I'm holding for it, holding for it, and then I start to get nervous that I'm going to wait too long, so I say the next line. The piece ends and as we're walking backstage, he says, "You stupid sonofabitch! You stepped all over the laugh!" I'm no longer his son. I'm now his partner.

About a year later, my father is working the Lake Huntington Lodge during the summer and it's great for us, because we get a cottage, we see greenery and we get to swim in a lake. I decide to go see another act, some friends of my father who are working down the road at the Loch Sheldrake Hotel. Feeling like a big shot, I go backstage to say hello before the show and the straight man is absolutely panicked. He tells me, "My partner just had an ulcer attack and we have to do a show! I don't have anyone!" I tell him, "I can do the sketch with you." He asks, "What sketch do you know?" I say, "All of 'em." He says, "Do you know 'I Got Twenty, You Got Twenty Too'?" I tell him, "Sure." He asks, "What about 'Joe the Bartender'?" I say, "I can do that, too." My father always asks for a derby and "a misfit jacket," because the sleeves are too long. I tell this guy, "I need a misfit jacket." Of course at my age, *any* jacket is a misfit jacket. I do the sketches with him and the show goes great. He's in shock that I know all the routines, but it's my life. It's all I want. Decades later, my dad and I perform those same pieces on *The Merv Griffin Show*.

I have a very good relationship with my father. I like him a lot, I admire him and I'm a little in awe of him. But as I grow older, I start to realize that he really does nothing to contribute to the family. When he isn't working, he isn't working. He doesn't find some kind of job to bring money in, so my mother handles all of it and pays all the bills. Every day, my father gets dressed up, fixes his tie, puts his suit on and goes uptown. My mother gives him five dollars for the week in allowance, because she's usually the one who's working. Sometimes, my brother accompanies him. My father gives a dollar to every down-on-his-luck performer he runs into, to make himself look like a big shot. Eddie is furious at my father's irresponsibility. He never really forgives him for that.

When I'm about nine, I'm walking past a Thom McCan shoe store on Delancey Street and see a pair of Boy Scout boots in the window. They come to just above the ankle and they have a pocket with a Boy Scout knife inside it. The boots are four dollars. Back then, shoes cost two dollars, but I *really* want those boots. I know that if I ask my mother, she'll say no, because there isn't enough money. I wait until my father's home, knowing he'll say, "Give him the boots." At the dinner table, I announce that I want the boots. My mother asks, "How much are they?" I say, "Four dollars." She says, "Are you out of your mind? Who ever heard of spending *four dollars* for shoes? That's ridiculous!" My father tells her, "Get him the boots." She says, "Jack, we don't have the money." He says, "I don't understand that. What do you mean we don't have the money?" She says, "We don't have the money to pay the rent, can you understand that?" He asks, "When is the rent due?" She says, "Tomorrow." He says, "Well then why are you worrying about it today?" Even at nine, I know there's something wrong with his logic, but that's the sort of man he is.

My father wins that round. We go to Thom McCan's, the salesman brings out the boots and I put them on, ecstatic. My mother asks, "What's in the pocket?" The salesman says, "That's an *official* Boy Scout knife!" My mother says, "That's it. Boots off. No knives. Forget about it. No boots." I go nuts: "Waaaa! I want my boots! I want my boots!" My father says, "Let's calm down and let's work this out. Supposing he agrees not to take the knife out of the boots. Will that work?" She looks at me and says, "You will not take the knife out of the boots?" I tell her, "I promise!" I *know* I'm not going to take the knife out of the boots, because she'll kill me. My mother thinks it over, says, "Okay," and I get the boots.

A couple of days later, my friend Victor Nagara and I find an old beat-up black leather attaché case near our school and Victor uses it to cut out Zorro masks for us. He hands me my mask, but the holes for the eyes are too small. I ask him, "Can you make the eyes a little bigger?" He tells me, "*You* got a knife. *You* do it." I'm not going to tell him my mother says I can't use the knife. What am I, a sissy? I take the knife out of the boot and open it up very carefully, but somehow the blade folds over, cutting deeply into the index finger of my left hand. It's a real gusher.

I walk up to the teacher and she faints. Somebody runs and gets the nurse. She treats the gash, then wraps a big, white gauze bandage around my finger that makes it look like a light bulb. I go home for lunch and I'm left-handed, but because of the cut, I'm eating with my right hand. My mother asks, "Why are you eating with your right hand?" I tell her, "Oh, I'm trying to learn to eat with my right hand." She says, "You took that *knife* out, didn't you?" She knows immediately. My mother is great with a dishtowel. She can snap it and take your eye out. She starts snapping the towel at me and screaming, "You sonofabitch! I *told* you not take the knife out! I *knew* this would happen!" I'm crying, "Ma! Ma! No! Please!" But that's the end of my boots. They're taken away from me and never given back.

I still have a scar on my left index finger from that official Boy Scout knife.

CHAPTER THREE

My maternal grandmother, Mary, is quite a character. Before she comes to America from Poland, she's already been married and divorced twice and has a son with each of her two Polish husbands. She's about to leave Poland with both boys when her first husband stops her and says, "You're not leaving with my son," and he takes the older boy. So she leaves Poland with only my Uncle Harry. They come to the United States and she has no idea where her older son is or what's going on with him.

One day, she's walking down the street in New York and she runs into a woman who has just arrived from Poland. She tells my grandmother, "I saw your son and his family." Mary gets the information and sends money to her son, who has become a gangster in Poland. His name is Menke – Menke the *shtarker*, the tough guy. She sends for Menke, who comes to New York with his wife and three children, my cousins Abie, Harry and Bessie. Later, he has two more children, cousin Sylvia and the youngest, cousin Bernice.

In 1931 – the year I'm born – Menke shoots and kills a mob guy on Essex Street, so the mob is looking for him. The guy he kills is with a gang run by Longie Zwillman, who controls New Jersey. He's a Jewish mobster, about six-feet-two, and because he's tall, they call him Longie. My father knows him, so he hides Menke in the Catskill Mountains, then goes to Jersey and has a meeting with Zwillman to tell him that this is his nephew and the guy had done such-and-such and that's why Menke shot him. Because of my father's intercession, Zwillman lets Menke off the hook – for the time being.

A year later, they lure Menke into a phony card game in Brooklyn, tie him in a blanket, pour gasoline on him, and light him up. My poor mother goes to the hospital to see him while he's still alive and he dies a short time later. Menke's wife died of cancer sometime earlier, so my mother takes in *all four* of her half-brother's children, two girls and two boys. To his credit, my father is very open to having them all come live with us. Of all the children, Bernice is the one who stays the longest.

When I'm about six or seven, Bernice's older brother, Harry, gets a job riding a horse and buggy, and he passes by the house at the end of the day to bring the horses to the stables on Cherry Street. I wait for him and I hop on and he lets me hold the reins. We ride to the stable and then we walk back home together. It's great fun!

When my cousin Abie gets married, his wife, Frances, stays at our house. As a kid, I'm in love with her. Abie is a great guy. When *Gone With The Wind* opens, they raise the price of a ticket from ten to twenty-five cents. I have no idea what the movie is about, but I know it's important and I want to see it, so I ask my mother if I can have a quarter. She says, "Who ever paid twenty-five cents for a movie? That's crazy!" But my cousin Abie gives me a quarter, so I get to see *Gone With The Wind*. He also buys me a cowboy outfit for my birthday. It has fur chaps, a plaid shirt, a cowboy hat and two guns. I love that outfit!

In the early '40s, when she's about eighteen, Bernice gets a job as an usherette at the Paramount Theatre. She meets Pigmeat Markham there – the black "Here come da judge!" comedian – and they get married. Everybody but my mother disowns Bernice for marrying a black man. They cut her off.

Bernice has two children with Pigmeat, a boy, Dewey – which is Pigmeat's real name – and a girl, Cathy. When Dewey is about two, I go up to Harlem, pick him up and take him to Central Park. We go to the zoo and we get a rowboat. My brother Eddie has a great sense of humor. One day, he takes Dewey home with him to Syosset, where Eddie is living. Dewey is playing in the backyard and a neighbor calls my brother and says, "There's a colored kid in your backyard." Eddie tells him, "Yeah, I know. It's a major problem for me. He's my wife's child from her first marriage and she *insists* on bringing him out here."

Pigmeat Markham is a brilliant comic. We have Thanksgiving dinner together. The whole family goes up to Bernice's in Harlem. My father and Pigmeat have a lot in common – except that Pigmeat works the Chitlin' Circuit and my father works the vaudeville houses and in burlesque. But they're both performers and the two of them go at it, telling story after story. It's great listening to the two of them swapping show-biz tales.

Pigmeat never lets his agent meet Bernice. Since agents are usually Jewish white guys who don't live in Harlem, he worries that if his agent finds out about Bernice, he won't get work. When the younger black comics like Dick Gregory are coming in, they attack the older black comics, calling them Uncle Toms and condemning them for wearing blackface, even though that was the accepted style in vaudeville. As a result, the older black comics can't get jobs. After a while, Pigmeat is broke.

At the time, my brother Eddie has a route delivering Mission Sodas to different groceries and candy stores in Harlem. He starts out with one truck and he ends up with three and a partner. They basically have the whole New York area. My mother tells my brother to ask around and find out where Bernice is, because she knows Bernice and Pigmeat are having a rough time making ends meet. Eddie finds the apartment and goes to visit her. I remember him telling us, "They're sleeping on a mattress with bricks holding the mattress up." As he leaves their place, Eddie puts a $20 bill on the table. My mother takes the train up from the Lower East Side, stops at a grocery in Harlem, buys loads of food and brings it to them. She does this once a week, but it's still very rough going for many years.

In 1968, Flip Wilson goes on *Laugh-In* and does Pigmeat's trademark bit: "Here come da judge!" Later, Sammy Davis Jr. does the same bit. Some comics contact the producer, George Schlatter, and tell him he can't do that to Pigmeat, who has been struggling for such a long time. Schlatter brings Pigmeat on the show for an entire season and he's just hilarious. Because of *Laugh-In*, Pigmeat gets *The Ed Sullivan Show*. I remember Bernice asking me if I can lend her fifty dollars so Pigmeat can buy a suit to do the show. Of course, I lend her the money.

Their son Dewey goes on to become a world-renowned wine connoisseur who lives in Bordeaux, takes people on tours of the vineyards and writes a book on wine that James Beard absolutely raves about. It's strange how things work out sometimes.

After my grandmother Mary comes to America, she marries a man named Penn and they become my maternal grandparents. They have a son named Moe, who is my mother's full-blooded brother. He owns a store that sells hats that mob guys just love. Years later, I'm working as a comic in Pittsburgh and I see a guy take off his hat. I notice the label says "Moe Penn" and I say, "Moe Penn. That's my uncle." The guys says, "You're kiddin' me! These are the best hats. I order six of 'em at a time. They ship 'em out to me. C'mere! What do you want? You want a steak? Give him whatever he wants."

When she's in her seventies, my mother finally reveals that when she was four, she's sitting on the fire escape with another brother who's two years old. None of us knew she ever had another brother besides Moe. He starts to fall off the fire escape and she's holding his leg, but she can't hang on and he falls to his death. My mother carries that guilt with her all those years – but it explains why she always makes such a big fuss over Uncle Moe.

In the early '30s, some mob guys put my father in business. He's out doing his comedy act wherever he can, but he's never very successful, so they tell him, "We're gonna open a haberdashery store on East Broadway. You run it and we'll run bookmaking and numbers in the back." My mother tells my father, "Take in my brother Moe. Make him a partner." Since my father has no interest in business, he says, "Fine." They call the haberdashery store "Moe-Jack's." Uncle Moe handles the buying and paying the bills, and my father is the charmer with the customers out front.

One day, a mob guy comes in and orders half a dozen custom-made silk shirts, but my father doesn't put the order in. The guy calls a month later, "What's happening with my shirts?" My father tells him, "Oh, they're working on it. I'll have 'em in a week." He keeps stalling, because he figures, "This guy is going to get killed in a week, so why bother making the shirts? I'll just hold on to the money!" One mob guy puts in an order for silk underwear, because he's cold all the time, then he gets shot to death on Delancey Street. My father saved the money on that one.

Eventually, my father and Uncle Moe start to get calls from the factory saying they haven't been paid. My uncle is getting shipments of material from the factory, but he isn't paying for it. My father's sister, Aunt Bea, has a husband who's a CPA. He looks the books over and tells my father, "Walk away. You're in a lot of trouble if you don't. Moe's never paid any of these bills. All that money is owed." They close the store down. A month later, Moe Penn opens up his hat store. Where did the money come from? My mother never complains and my father couldn't care less. Give him a stage and a microphone and he's a happy man. Moe's business begins to thrive and eventually becomes very successful, although he owes everybody money, because that's the kind of guy he is.

Eventually, Moe gets cancer and dies at the age of 58. His wife can't handle that he's dying, so my mother moves in with them, sleeps in the bed with my uncle, nurses him and takes care of him in his final days.

She really is the matriarch of the family.

CHAPTER FOUR

During the Depression, my mother works hard at Schrafft's Restaurant washing dishes. She controls the family money – however much there is. Because money is always so tight, she gets very frustrated and beats the shit out of me. If that were to happen today, she would go to jail. I admit I'd usually done something wrong, but it doesn't warrant that kind of attack. It's all anger and frustration at my father. She never hits my brother Eddie. She adores him. Eddie is the first son, so he chooses to be the good son. I come along and that part is taken, so I decide, not consciously, to be the difficult one. I'm always in trouble. My mother says, "If there's a fight in the street, I can guarantee you Howard's in the middle of it." I rebel against everything. Sometimes, my mother starts to discipline me by saying, "Howard, you'll *rue the day*..." but I interrupt with, "Ma, we're not English!"

This isn't to say my mother is against my getting into fights. One day in fifth grade, I come home from school for lunch and I get my usual meal – spinach and potatoes. It's cheap and delicious. I tell my mother I have a stomachache and I can't go back to school. She says, "I know you. You don't have a stomachache. What's going on?" She gets me to confess: "This kid chased me home from school." She tells me, "Well, you can't not go to school, so go back to school. If he doesn't bother you again, ignore it. If he bothers you, you fight him as hard as you can. You don't have to win, but I promise you, he'll never bother you again." I ask her why, and she tells me, "Because nobody likes to get hit."

I walk back to school looking between every car. I'm hoping that kid fell off a roof, maybe he got hit by a truck, *anything* so I don't have to face him. I come up the school steps and get in line outside our homeroom and I'm watching every kid that comes through the door. Finally he shows, but by the time I see him, I've worked myself up to the point that as soon as I see his face, I scream "Ahhhh!!!!"

and I go running at him. I dive at him and knock him down and I beat the living shit out of him. They have to peel me off of him, because I just go nuts! But that's the end of it. He never bothers me again. My mother is right: Nobody likes to get hit. I'm very much like my mother: Always a ringleader, always stepping up and doing what has to be done. I think I inherited that from her. I mean, she made me go back and fight that bully!

I'm tough, but I'm also a sickly child. Every winter, my glands swell – neck, under the arms, groin – and I wind up in Beth Israel Hospital for two weeks and then in a convalescent home. At one point, the settlement houses in the greater New York area are looking for seventy-five underprivileged children to go to winter camp. I'm one of the kids that gets to go. Later, I realize why: My mother can't go to work and make a living if I'm running around the streets. She'd worry. My brother is fifteen and I'm ten. He's okay. He can handle himself. But they think it best for me to go to this camp. It's at Surprise Lake in Cold Springs, New York. Later, I do a joke in my act: "We were so poor, I went to *winter* camp."

At camp, the downstairs dining room is the dormitory. There are 75 of us down there, ranging in age from ten to fourteen. We have cots and go to classes and our teacher is Miss Canary. There's one fourteen-year-old – his last name is Shoemaker. He comes into the bathroom and catches a ten- or eleven-year-old alone and beats the hell out of him. One day, he does it to me, so I organize four other kids and I tell them, "After lights out, we all meet in the bathroom. Bring your slippers, 'cause we're gonna beat the hell out of him." So that's what we do. He's half-asleep and we attack him with the slippers. He looks up at me and I tell him, "If you hit any of us again, you will not sleep another night." Sure enough, he backs off.

At camp, a kid named Myron is picking on my friend, Reuben, who is not a fighter. He's a quiet kid. I know if I hit Myron, they'll make us fight the next day, because if you have any kind of a problem, they pull you apart and you get in the ring with gloves on. One day, Myron hits Reuben on the head with a bottle of something called Dope, which is glue for model airplanes. The glass doesn't break, but it really hurts him, so I go over and punch Myron and start to fight, knowing I'll have to fight him in the ring. We fight the next day – and I exact my revenge.

One day, they tell us "Henry Aldrich" is going to visit us at camp. We all listen to *The Aldrich Family* radio show: "Henry! Henry Aldrich!" "Coming, Mother!" We're all excited, but we have an image of Henry Aldrich as a sixteen-year-old kid. On the radio, he's played by an actor named Ezra Stone, who later becomes a director. The day arrives and we're all standing outside, eagerly awaiting the arrival of Henry Aldrich. A station wagon pulls up and this balding guy, heavyset, about thirty-five years old, gets out. We start screaming at him, "You're not Henry Aldrich! They lied to us! That's not Henry Aldrich!" We *know* Henry Aldrich is sixteen and here's this thirty-five-year-old, balding guy with red hair. The poor man. He comes to do a good deed and we attack him!

When I'm around twelve, I catch a thing called "Huntington's chorea." It's what Woody Guthrie died from. There are two forms of it: One is deadly and is also known as St. Vitus' Dance, and the other isn't. I'm lucky enough to have the other, which causes you to lose control of your nerves. We're in the Catskill Mountains and my father is working a place called – coincidentally – The Huntington Lodge in Lake Huntington. My mother asks, "Why are you making faces? What's with the faces?" I'm twitching, but I have no idea I'm doing anything. Then my walk starts to get strange, like a shuffle, and she asks me, "What's with the funny walk? Why are you walking like that?" At first, they don't understand, but then they realized something was really wrong with me.

They take me to a camp where a doctor examines me for polio, but that isn't the problem. They finally figure out it's some kind of nerve thing. This is a really terrible time in my life. I'm put into a dark room – no stimulation, meaning I can't read and I can't listen to the radio. I have to just lie in bed and take this sedative, a red liquid in a bottle. I'm going nuts having to lie there all day and do nothing.

My great aunt Jenny, my father's aunt, is a real character; very funny. She's staying in the Catskills and she comes to visit me every day. She takes a wire hanger and puts it around her neck like it's a stethoscope. She examines me with it and then she says, "Sonny boy, I got bad news. You're pregnant." Every time she visits, she leaves a dollar. I save up all those dollars to make an escape, because I can't stand it anymore. I put all this money together – about seventeen dollars – and I start to run down the road. My sister Sylvia sees me running and she starts screaming. A handyman from one of the hotels sees me running and hears my sister screaming, so he grabs me. I start punching him and kicking him and Sylvia is yelling, "Come back! Mom will kill me!" I settle down, because I realize she's right. My mother will kill her, will beat the living daylights out of her, because she let me run away. So – back to bed I go. This goes on for months. I eventually get to go home, but I still have to take six months off from school. I sit in front of my building and watch all my friends playing stickball and coming home from school. It's a very tough time for me.

During the war, Sylvia, now eighteen, married a guy named Lenny, who's twenty-one. They knew each other a total of six months: Three months of dating, then they get married, then they're together as husband and wife for three months until he gets drafted. They live on Rutgers Street, just around the corner from us. Lenny gets wounded in the Aleutian Islands, then he's sent to Hawaii to recuperate, and then he's sent back into action and is killed in Leyte.

I will never forget the day we found out. So many American soldiers are being killed, the Western Union guys delivering telegrams can't handle it anymore. They go to an address, knock on the door, give them the telegram, and then they hear screaming and wailing and people fainting. They don't want to deliver telegrams anymore, so they start delivering them to the super or anybody else but the immediate family. In our case, the messenger delivers it to the super, but the super won't come up and deliver it, so he goes across the street and gives it to my uncle.

Nobody ever gets telegrams in that neighborhood, so you don't have to open it to know what it says: "Your son is dead or missing in action" or whatever. My uncle calls my mother, who goes to see him across the street. We're in the back room and I'm around thirteen at the time. I remember hearing my mother screaming in the street. My brother and I get up and she comes running into the house. As soon as we hear her screaming, Sylvia starts screaming, so Eddie and I try to deal with both of them. Then the neighbors come. Everybody is trying to settle them down. A little old Italian woman from the fifth floor, who always wears black, comes in, speaks no English, then takes some washcloths and pours vinegar and water on them. Then she puts them on the foreheads of my mother and my sister, who are just going nuts. They're screaming. Sylvia tries to jump out the window, so we quickly grab her. It's a crazy, horrible scene.

The old Italian woman goes all around the kitchen, doing whatever she can, and then she disappears back upstairs. Later on, we realize she's made a complete stew from whatever we have in the refrigerator. It's on the burner simmering, so we'll have something to eat that night. An absolutely amazing, beautiful, selfless gesture.

CHAPTER FIVE

The Lewis brothers are tough guys. They're like vigilantes. There's Jerry and his brother Lenny, Lee Hirsch and a guy we called Fumfy, because he fumfered when he talked. They find out a guy got beat up because he's Jewish and they go and find the guys that did it. They stand back-to-back in the street and take on ten or twelve guys. The Lewis brothers are some heavy-duty Jews. Everybody thinks of Jews as being passive and never fighting. Growing up in my neighborhood, I find just the opposite. We have Jewish guys that fight anytime anybody says anything about the Jews.

There's a kid named Kibbee Weinberg who comes down to the corner to get us if he needs help. One day, Kibbee comes down to the corner and he says, "Four guys took a kid's yarmulke. I want to get it back. I'm gonna fight one of them, but make sure the other three don't jump me." We walk up to the middle of the block and Kibbee tells the four guys, "Who's your best fighter?" They say, "Carmine." Kibbee says, "Okay, me and you for the yarmulke!" Kibbee takes his yarmulke off and slips it in his back pocket with his right hand, and while the guy is distracted by the yarmulke, Kibbee hits him with a left hook. Wham!

That's my neighborhood. There's definitely an element of danger there, but there's also an unwritten code of respect and decency. Nobody ever insults anybody's mother. You do that and it's over. You respect elderly people. My mother tells me that if I see an older person with a grocery bag, I should go and help them – and if I don't, I'll hear about it.

My neighborhood has a bunch of very tough Jewish guys. Some of them are gangsters, really. Among them is a seventeen-year-old kid who, many years later (and much to my surprise) becomes one of my closest friends – Seymour Rand. I don't like the people he hangs out with and I don't like what they're doing. They're already sticking up joints at seventeen and I have no interest in hanging around with him.

In 1985, John Gotti takes over the Gambino family, which, by now, includes Seymour, because he's such a big earner. The FBI is taking pictures of Gotti all the time: videos, photos, surveillance. Seymour is walking out of the Ravenite club with Gotti one day and he says, "John, those guys on those lampposts, they're not electricians. That's FBI." Gotti says, "Fuck 'em."

There's a made man that's Gotti's guy, and when they are all walking out of the Ravenite, the guy is making anti-Semitic remarks to Seymour. Seymour turns on him and he waves his finger in his face, saying, "I know you're a made man and if I kill you, I'm gonna get killed, but I'm willing to die. Are *you*?!" Gotti says, "Seymour! Take it easy!" The FBI sees this guy wagging his finger at a made man. They say, "Who the fuck is this guy? He must be major!" So they go after Seymour. They put a bug in his car and in his house. My closest friend, Billy Fields, is on those tapes talking to Seymour. It's through Billy that I reconnect with Seymour all those years after our rough-and-tumble childhood.

The FBI nails Seymour on a RICO act. It's the first time in the history of the RICO act they make it a state case instead of federal, because he won't turn Gotti over. He could have very easily, because everybody else does, but Seymour's sense of honor won't let him. He refuses to turn Gotti over. When you're up on a RICO thing, they tie up everything you have. They get your money, your house, your cars – whether you're guilty or not. They lock it all up, because their claim is that all the money came from racketeering. I run into another guy who's the token Jew with the Genovese mob, a guy named Charlie Waxman. He tells me, "Y'know, John didn't like Seymour." I tell him, "Yeah, but he liked how much money he brought in and he also liked the fact that Seymour was the only guy that didn't turn on him." Charlie says, "You're right. All the Italians turned on him. The one Jew stood up."

Seymour goes to jail. He does a lot of time at Riker's during the trial, then they move him. I think he does a total of three years. Two years are at Collins Correctional Facility above Buffalo. Billy goes to visit him there. Seymour tells Billy, "Do me a favor. I need to be sure my family gets taken care of, so I'm gonna make you a partner in my bookmaking business. I don't want you shylocking, because I don't want you to have to deal with that." Seymour is a *shtarker*, a tough guy. When you're shylocking and they don't pay you, you break their legs or you threaten them. Seymour does that, but on his own.

Seymour's bail is $750,000. It's a *cash* bail, because the FBI is so pissed at him, they get the judge to make it so you have to come up with all that money at once. Billy goes around to everybody they know and gets enough money together to cover Seymour's bail. One guy comes up with 250 thou, and he's a legitimate business guy – he and Seymour aren't even close friends. Eventually, everybody gets his money back. Seymour tells Billy, "Now that you're a partner in the business, make sure Harriet and the kids are taken care of." Knowing Billy, whenever they lose money, Billy goes to Harriet and gives her enough money for the week or the month.

While Seymour's in prison, Gotti wants to thank him. He contacts Buffalo and asks the mob guys there if they know anybody in that prison. They say, "Yeah, we know a couple of guys." Gotti says, "I want them to protect this guy, Seymour. He's a stand-up guy." On Seymour's first day in prison, he decides he's not going to make friends with anybody; he's just going to do his two years. He says, "I'll just read my books and I'll stay out of trouble. I don't need friends." He's sitting at a table in the yard, reading, and a young guy comes up and says, "How you doing, Pop?" Seymour is fifty-eight at the time. He answers, "Fine." The guy says, "We heard what you did for John, so if you need anything, let us know, and just know we got your back, okay?" and he leaves two cigarettes. Next day, another guy shows up, same story, he leaves chewing gum. Third day, another guy comes, same thing, and leaves a candy bar. A week passes and they come to Seymour and tell him, "Stay out of the yard tomorrow." He says, "Okay" and he stays in his cell. That day, they kill a guy in the yard. They didn't want Seymour anywhere near that.

He does his time, gets out, and goes back to bookmaking and partners with Billy. Sometime later, Billy is having lunch with Seymour in New York and Seymour invites a friend who just got out of jail. The minute lunch is over, Billy calls me and says, "I just had lunch with a friend of Seymour's, an ex-con. The guy says, 'I've been out of the can for three months. I got the New York Police force on my ass, I got the New York District Attorney on my ass, and the FBI on my ass. They're trying to nail me for ten murders. Ten murders!?! Nowhere *near*!'"

Eventually, Seymour retires, Billy buys him out and that's that. He moves to Florida with his wife, Harriet. Nowadays, you mention Seymour's grandchildren to him and he's just a big pussycat.

But that wasn't the case when we were kids...

CHAPTER SIX

Joe Louis isn't from our neighborhood, but he's everybody's boxing hero. Whenever Louis is fighting, someone runs a wire up to
their apartment and plugs in the radio. We have the radio sitting
on the stoop and we all stand around, listening to the fight. I love
listening to the radio, but the thing that always seems strange to me
is that we all gather around the radio and *stare* at it, as if Joe Louis
or Jack Benny were inside it or something. Do we know television
is coming? Jack Benny is my favorite radio show. He's the bravest
comic I've ever known, because he'll wait out a laugh for a week if
necessary. I also love Fred Allen. He once said, "You can take all
the sincerity in Hollywood, put it in the navel of a flea, and still
have room for three caraway seeds and the heart of an agent." The
thought process behind that is just brilliant.

For movies, James Cagney is my hero. I love him, because he also
comes from the streets, from Germantown up around 2nd Avenue,
86th Street. And, of course, the Dead End Kids movies are great.
A favorite is *Angels With Dirty Faces* with Jimmy Cagney and Pat
O'Brien, where O'Brien becomes the priest and Cagney becomes
the gangster. For actresses, I'm madly in love with Gene Tierney
and Ann Sheridan.

When it comes to movie comedy, I love the Marx Brothers. Out
of all of them, my favorite is Harpo. Jack Oakie is one of the great
comedy actors. In fact, Jackie Gleason does a lot of Oakie. Oakie is
always the second banana, but he's very solid. He's never the lead
performer like Gleason on his television series and in movies. He
knows where the laughs are and how to get them, and he's kind of
brash, like Gleason.

I also love the Ritz Brothers. Their movies aren't very good, but
I love what they do. The dancing in unison is great and Harry is
brilliant. Most of the stuff Jerry Lewis does is Harry Ritz. Danny
Kaye is my favorite performer. His wife, Sylvia Fine, writes brilliant

lyrics, brilliant stuff for him. Without her, I don't think he would be the star he is. When I get older, I'm not as impressed with him, because I think he's a very talented performer, but I didn't really think he's *funny*.

Later on, in television, there's Milton Berle and *The Ed Sullivan Show*, and Sid Caesar to me is the best sketch comic that ever lived. There's no one better than Caesar. The only one that comes close is Jackie Gleason. Caesar and Gleason are great in sketches, but bad at standup.

My favorite standup is a guy named Jackie Miles. I see him at the Paramount Theatre and again in the Catskills. Unlike a lot of rapid-fire standups, he's very low-key. If the audience gets noisy, he gets quieter until they start to lean in. He does a piece I love. In those days, you go into a movie theatre whenever you feel like going in; you don't have to see the movie from the beginning. Miles does a routine where one guy says, "This is where we came in," and the other guy says, "Nah, this isn't where we came in." That's always the argument. You go in with three or four friends and they wind up arguing about it. Jackie says, "Don't you remember the guy with the moustache gets shot?" and he does this whole routine. It's all very original. I also admire Phil Foster and Jan Murray a lot and, of course, Dean Martin and Jerry Lewis are brilliant. Their chemistry is unbelievable.

I'm in love with show business from the time I'm an infant. My friend Marty Nedboy also loves show business. When we're about thirteen, we take the F train uptown to 50th Street every Saturday, then walk around looking at marquees and figuring out what we want to see, even though we don't have any money. We pick a show and wait for intermission and we hang out with the audience, who's talking and smoking and milling around. Once intermission is over and the audience goes back in, we walk in with them and find a couple of empty seats. We always see the last act of a play. We never get to see the first act.

One day, I tell Marty, "That's it. This Saturday, we're gonna see a *whole show*. I'll jimmy a door and we'll sneak in." We go to the Winter Garden Theatre and the marquee says *Laffing Room Only*, which immediately gets my attention. A sign says "Olsen & Johnson With

Betty Garrett." The theatre's back-door entrance is on 7th Avenue. Somehow, I find a way to get the door open and we walk in. We're not in the actual theatre; we're backstage. People are running around and moving scenery and it's all very exciting. Suddenly, a guy walks up to us and says, "What are you doing here?!" I see a picture of a woman and her name: "BETTY GARRETT." I tell him, "We came to see Betty Garrett." He says, "She better be expecting you."

He grabs both of us by our collars, walks us over to Betty Garrett's dressing room and knocks on the door. She says, "Yes?" He says, "Miss Garrett, there are two 'young men' out here I caught snooping around and they claim they have an appointment with you." She says, "Oh yes, I'm expecting them." We walk in and she closes the door. She's wearing a robe and putting her makeup on. She asks, "What's going on?" I tell her, "We never saw a whole play. We always sneak in and see the second act, but we never see a whole play." She tells us, "Come back next Saturday. There will be two tickets for you at the box-office. After the show, come backstage and say hello."

We're so excited about seeing the show, we cannot wait for the weekend. We go back to the Winter Garden and sure enough, there are the tickets. We see the whole play and we're in heaven. We go backstage afterward and we bring her a dozen day-old roses, because we can't afford fresh ones. She dresses and we walk her back to her apartment building on 8th Avenue around 53rd or 54th Street. We're invited upstairs and we're introduced to her mother, who pours us pineapple juice out of a cut-glass crystal pitcher that has matching glasses. Marty and I can't believe the glasses match the pitcher. We're used to drinking out of jelly jars or *yarzheit* candles, which are Jewish memorial candles.

Marty and I stay in touch with Betty. One time, she takes us to a radio show she's doing and we get to sit in the audience. Then she does a new play, *Call Me Mister*, co-starring Bill Callahan, about a guy who's returning from the war. Betty says, "If you want to see the play, call me and when you hear the overture, I'll come backstage and open the door. You run in and find seats." So we do it! She comes out in full costume, lets us in and we watch the show. She's this big Broadway star and she's so kind to us. I see the play maybe ten or fifteen times. I learn every song in the show. I want to *be* Bill Callahan. At the time, Betty's dating actor Larry Parks. In her dressing room is a life-sized cutout of Larry as Jolson in blackface from *The Jolson Story*. She's mad about him and it's great to see her so much in love.

Betty's going to do a radio show to plug *Call Me Mister* and I ask her, "Can you mention our names?" She says, "I'll try." The radio host asks her, "Who's in the cast?" and she says, "Well, there's Bill Callahan, Jules Munshin, Howie Sobel, Marty Nedboy..." We're listening to the radio and we hear our names! We just go *crazy!*

Time passes and we gradually lose touch. Years later, I'm directing *Laverne & Shirley*. The Executive Producer, Garry Marshall, tells me, "We're bringing in a woman to play the landlady." I ask him, "Who is it?" He says, "Betty Garrett." I don't say a word. I just wait. Monday read-through time and in comes Betty Garrett. I walk up to her and I say, "Miss Garrett, do you remember a kid named Howie Sobel?" She looks at me and says, "Oh my God! It's *you!* What are you doing here?" I tell her, "I'm the director."

After *Laverne & Shirley*, we remain friends for the rest of her life.

CHAPTER SEVEN

When I'm fourteen, I get a job after school and go to work for the *New York Post*. I grab a stack of papers, jump off the back of a truck, and drop the stack onto the sidewalk at newsstands and candy stores all around the area. My mother controls the money in the family and her rule is that you give her everything you earn and she gives you an allowance. I refuse, telling her, "I'm making the money. Tell me how much I owe and I'll give you that, but I'm not giving you all my money." To my relief, she's okay with that. I'm making fourteen dollars a week for the *New York Post* and I give her seven. The rent is thirty-two dollars a month and I'm contributing twenty-eight of it!

During the war, my mother leases a coffee shop in the Catskills. My sister remarries and her new husband manages a wholesale candy and tobacco business on Second Avenue. Two guys own it, but they do nothing, so he's basically in control. I get a hundred count of bubble gum for a dollar-ten and I sell them in junior high school for twenty-five cents apiece. Nobody can get gum during the war, not even the candy store, but my brother-in-law gets it for me and I sell it at school – until the principal finds out and tells me I can't sell it on the property. So I wait on the corner near the school and everybody comes running. If you don't have a quarter, my rates are reasonable – I'll take a dime, I'll take fifteen cents, whatever you have. I make a load of money selling bubble gum and I *don't* turn it over to my mother. That's mine.

My brother-in-law can also get us cigarettes, which are impossible to get. In those days, candy stores take a pack of cigarettes, tear them open – which is illegal – and sell them loose. No one can afford the ten cents for an entire pack, so they buy one or two at a time for a penny each. We called them loosies. There's a candy store, a barbershop, and a Chinese laundry right under where we live on the first floor. Sam Lee, the laundryman, is very nice. He gives me

lichee nuts and teaches me how to write in Chinese. Sam the Barber tells me, "Do me a favor, Howie. Get a couple of loosies." I go
next door and buy two cigarettes for him, so the owner of the candy
store makes twenty cents instead of ten. It's a little like the black
market.

My parents are able to get candy, sugar, cigars and cigarettes,
which are otherwise impossible to find. They accumulate some real
money from this business, which goes on for two summers. Once
they have a little money, my mother becomes another person. She
settles down and the beatings subside.

Shortly after the war ends, my father needs to have a kidney
removed, which is literally a major operation in those days. He figures he can find work in Miami while he's recuperating and that it
will benefit us to be there, so I leave high school and we go to Florida. Eddie is still in the army and Sylvia has remarried, so they're
both out of the nest.

Despite my father's high hopes, my parents have a very difficult
time in Florida. For me, however, Miami is of great significance,
because that's where I meet up with my first performing partner,
Lou Gostel, later known as Lou Alexander. Lou's father, Jo-Jo
Gostel, works as a burlesque comic in a club called Zissen's Bowery,
which is a really seedy, bust-out kind of a club. As women walk in,
an air hose in the floor blows their skirts up. The performers have
to wait on tables when they aren't performing, which is humiliating
for my father. Zissen's has a big washbasin on the stage and people
throw money into it. If they like you, you get more money, and then
it's split among all the performers. They also have to wear T-shirts
that say "Zissen's Bowery" on them. We live above the club. I have a
room and my parents have one large room with a table, chairs and
a hotplate. Lou's father also has two rooms, and he's living with a
beautiful young woman named Linda.

Lou and I get on the bus to take us to Edison High School, the
last stop on the bus, and it's like being in Mississippi or Alabama.
We're two New York Jews thrown into this school with every anti-
Semite Southern bigot that you can think of. We get into a *lot* of
fights. I remember a football player with a cast on his leg who says

something insulting to me, so I kick his good foot out from under him and down he goes. I don't stick around.

One day, I get on the public bus and this one kid says, "That's my seat." I tell him, "What do you mean it's your seat? This is a public bus. These are not assigned seats." He says, "That's my seat." I refuse to get up and we get into a fight. A group of kids threaten to come back and get us later that day. Next to Zissen's is a big pit, with gravel piled about a story high. I climb up on top of it with Lou, who has his father's .22 rifle. We're waiting for them to show up when Lou's father spots us and says, "What are you doin' with that rifle?" We tell him these guys are coming to get us and he says, "What're you gonna do, shoot 'em and kill 'em?!" He gives Lou a whack on the back of the head, grabs the gun and tells him, "Get back upstairs!"

Lou and I hate school and we decide we aren't going back there anymore, so every morning, we get on the bus and when it gets to the last stop, Edison High, we slide down in our seats and hide. The bus turns around and goes into Miami. We get there about 9:00 or 9:30 and since the movies aren't open yet, there are two places we go. One is Lionel Trains, because we love to watch the model trains zooming around the track. The other is a magic shop. We go in and ask the guy, "How does this trick work?" and he does tricks. He does a whole magic show, just for us!

Then we get a piece of delicious Boston cream pie in a little café that's upstairs at Whelan's Drugstore. When it's time, we go buy a ticket to a movie and a show at the Olympic Theatre. They have vaudeville, like the New York Paramount; live shows and performers in addition to the movie. We *love* watching those performers. That's when Lou and I decide we're going into show business together.

When Lou and I start out, we do one or two dates for nothing – but we actually have a writer. Jules Zissen is the hunchbacked nephew of the owner of the Bowery. He's concerned about having one of us named Louis – because of Martin & Lewis – so we become Howard & Lawrence. We only do one or two little things for no money, but we are performing material written just for us.

There's an old alcoholic custodian named Pat O'Brien, who cleans and sweeps out Zissen's Bowery. Since our mail comes to the club and Pat's around all day, Lou and I give him a dollar a week to take our truant notices and throw them away! He does this for about three months. One day, I'm having dinner in my parents' little apartment and there's a knock at the door. My mother says, "Come in." Jo-Jo Gostel has Lou by the ear and they're with a tall woman, a truant officer. Jo-Jo points at Lou and says, "If *he's* not going to school, that means *he's* not going to school," pointing at me. "They're *both* playing hooky." I'm busted.

We find out later that the school lost my files. They don't even know I exist, so I never get a truant notice. All the truant notices that Pat O'Brien throws away come for Lou. There's a big meeting and my father and mother come to the school. At first, we go in together, then Lou and I are told to leave and there is a private meeting between the parents. On the way home, my father tells me, "There's a law in Florida that if a child doesn't go to school, they arrest the parents. If you don't go back, Mom and I could go to jail." This is *total* bullshit, of course, but he's really good at that. So back to Edison High I go – until another significant incident occurs.

Linda, the woman who lives with Lou's father, is a beautiful, thirty-one-year-old nymphomaniac who looks like Linda Darnell. At the same time, Jo-Jo is teaching a twenty-one-year-old Canadian girl named Pat how to be a striptease dancer. One night, Lou and I are in the room with Pat and Linda. While I'm wrestling on the bed with Pat, I find myself aroused and I wind up screwing her. Linda says, "I wish Jo-Jo was here. I am hot to trot." I tell her, "I'll do it." She agrees, so we go into the other room and I make love to her. It sounds unbelievable, but that is my first time: One night, fourteen years old, two beautiful women.

Linda gets nervous and worries that I might tell my parents what happened, so to protect herself, she tells them she caught me with Pat. I'm so angry, I tell my parents the truth, but I don't tell them the part about screwing Linda, because I'm afraid for Jo-Jo. Eddie has come to visit us in Florida. I remember him standing there in his uniform. My father is worried about me getting a disease and he asks me, "Did you use anything? Do you know what a condom is?" Before I can answer, my brother says, "Of course, he knows what a condom is." My father asks me, "Did you use one?" I blurt out, "Yes!

It was *Linda* that gave it to me!" My mother promptly announces, "That's it. We're going home." She tells Jo-Jo, "This is not an environment for a young man. Your son is going with us." We get in the car, which is jammed with all of our belongings, we drive back to New York and we take Lou to his Aunt Lily's house. After five months in Florida, we're back in our Henry Street apartment on the Lower East Side.

CHAPTER EIGHT

After all the lousy breaks, my father finally gets lucky. When he's in the Catskills, there's a young college kid who loves show business. He asks my father if he can get a job building sets or doing pretty much anything just to be around it. My father is very kind to him. The guy becomes a lawyer and years later, he's the in-house attorney for BMI – Broadcast Music Incorporated – which represents song rights for composers.

After we get back from Florida, he calls my father and he says, "Jack, you know the Catskill Mountains very well. You know all the hotels. I can give you a job signing them up, contracts for BMI. It won't affect your performances at night. You can still do your act, but during the day, all you have to do is drive around to the different hotels. You *know* all those people." So that's what he does. My father literally signs up the entire Catskill Mountains for BMI!

Then BMI asks him if he wants to cover nightclubs in New York. He already knows all the mob guys, because he grew up with them. They're not going to throw him out on his ass when he walks into a club and says, "If you want to use music from BMI, you have to sign." Any other guy would get the shit beat out of him in the alley, but they all know him and like him. So he signs the New York clubs, and then they send him out to Pittsburgh for a week to hit a few places, and then on to Philadelphia. He does very well. He makes a good living and it's steady work. My father is *finally* bringing in decent money.

In the Catskills, every comic in every hotel does a one-night show where all the comics from the other hotels come to watch. They charge a dollar to see all these comedians at one time, and that money goes to the comic from that hotel. And then, in turn, he does the same thing for them. I remember seeing a fifteen-year-old Jerry Lewis doing an act where he's miming to records. That's how the comics functioned at the Catskill hotels.

Lou Alexander and I get our first job in the Catskills through my father. We each get $20 a week plus room and board to be assistants to the comic – Mac Dennison – and the singer/straight man – Georgie Tuttle. We help them in sketches if they need an extra person and we get to do a little bit of our own once in a while. That's our first paying job.

An agent offers my father a job in Boston at a club called The French Village in the basement of the Tremont Hotel. He doesn't really want it, so he "sells" us to the agent, saying, "I have two guys who would just be *terrific*." Now Lou and I *really* have a professional job. We're going to work in a nightclub. We get $150, which we split $75 and $75 and the club pays the agent. We go in for a week and we stay for *eight*. Our first nightclub job and we're a hit! We do a lot of old burlesque sketches that our fathers do. The audience is made up mostly of truckers who are driving eighteen-wheelers from Canada and Maine into New York, and they stop over in Boston to sleep for a night.

In one of our bits, I'm a veterinarian and Lou's a farmer. He says, "My mule is sick. I don't know what to do." I tell him, "Not a problem. You take this hose and you put it down the mule's esophagus and then you take this talcum powder and you pour it down the esophagus and then you blow on the tube to make sure the talcum powder spreads evenly. I assure you, that mule will be like new!" Lou says, "Okay!" and he goes offstage. I tell the audience, "You watch now. That mule will be as good as it's ever been. This is the perfect antidote." I'm filling time. Then from backstage, you hear the drum go bang, boom, crash! Lou comes walking out with his hair all messed up and talcum powder all over his face. I ask, "What happened?" and he says, "The mule blew first." Audiences love that kinda stuff.

The audience gets pretty drunk at the club, but Lou and I are fearless. If they heckle us, we go right back at them. Sometimes we stand on their tables and give them a lecture. "You don't heckle anybody! You're not supposed to do that!" They get hysterical. We climb up on the table, we pour beer on one guy, but they love that we have the kind of guts we have. The truth is, we aren't smart enough to know any better. We're just two cocky kids who think we're funny – and we stay at The French Village for eight weeks.

Lou and I are playing a club in Skowhegan, Maine, and I get into a beef with a lumberjack who heckles us. The guy is about six-four, two hundred and twenty pounds. He and I go outside, but the snow is so deep that when I step off the porch, I disappear up to my shoulders! I can't even get my arms out of the snow to fight! When he steps off, the snow only comes up to about his hips. Lou tells him, "Don't fight him!" The guy asks, "Why not?" Lou says, "'Cause you'll kill him and you'll wind up in jail for the rest of your life! Besides, I don't know how to do a single! I need someone to give me the lines!" The guy turns around and walks back into the club.

Our agent books us into the Shamrock Village, which is in Sullivan Square in the Charlestown neighborhood of Boston. The club itself was originally a garage, so they built the stage on two lifts. If you're sitting ringside when the stage comes up, it's higher than eye level. You have to lean back and look up to see what's going on. The club is owned by an Irish gangster whose girlfriend, Mavis, is the star of the show. She's knockout gorgeous: Blonde, beautiful, great dancer. Lou and I go in for a week and stay for four. We could've stayed longer, but when our agent says, "I can guarantee you a year's work," Lou tells him, "It's too cold here. I want to go back to Florida." So back to Florida we go.

Lou and I take our act to Florida, but we don't work for a long, long time and I go completely broke. By this time, Jo-Jo Gostel has left Linda and is living with another woman, so Lou stays with them. Jo-Jo finds me a garage that's been converted into a room and I share that with an old man for seven bucks a week. We're so broke, Lou and I take jobs in Dubrow's Cafeteria in Miami Beach. When someone fills their tray with food, we help them – usually elderly people – take the tray to the table, set everything up, bring them water, and they tip us.

We work at Dubrow's from four in the afternoon to eight at night for fifty cents an hour. With tips, we wind up making another four dollars, so we make eight bucks a day apiece, which is cool. We also wash silverware in the kitchen – but we always keep our tuxedoes in our locker, just in case we get a real job at a club. We finish work and go to see all the name comics that are in town. One night, we go to see Red Buttons. When the check comes, we don't have enough money to pay it, so we go backstage to Red's dressing room, introduce ourselves, tell him who our fathers are, and ask him if we can "borrow" ten dollars to pay the bill. Red gives us the ten and we pay the check. Years later, Red tells us that after we left his dressing room, he turned to his writer and said, "I'll never see those kids again." He was wrong: The next day, we come back and pay him the ten dollars.

Lou and I get booked in Key West. My job is to emcee the show and introduce the striptease dancers, and then at some point, we do our act. The first night, the room is 80% sailors, because ships have come into port. I walk out and before I can say a word, they start yelling, "Get off the stage! You stink! Bring on the strippers! Go back to high school!" Then they start shaking up their beer bottles and shpritzing me. I struggle through the first night, but the next day, I come up with an idea. I get a list of ships that are in town and I come out onstage and say, "I want to welcome *the battleship Pershing!*" They scream and applaud; just an unbelievable reaction. "And let's have a big hand for *the carrier U.S.S. Halsey!*" "Yayyyy!" They're screaming and cheering. This goes on every night. The owner of the club has a speaker in his office and he can hear all the cheering and applause and screaming, so he holds us over. I spend two weeks announcing ships.

I emcee the show and then I bring Lou out and we do our act. Basically, it's straight man and comic, but I also tell jokes in between acts, so I'm a comic doing standup, and then I'm a straight man for Lou. We do a routine where Lou is going to swim the English Channel. He comes out onstage with a robe and a shower cap on, and I ask, "Tell me, how did it go?" Lou says, "As you know, it's quite a distance, the Channel. I got halfway there and I got tired, so I turned back." Big laugh. Then he says, "As you know, you grease up your body." "As you know" is always the setup. "I got so much grease, I kept slipping off the water." That's one of the routines we do. We also do a Jekyll and Hyde bit where I mix all the chemicals and give Lou the stuff to drink and he drops behind the table and comes up as Mr. Hyde. We decide to call ourselves something that has a catchy sound, but we want to keep our actual initials – S & G – so we become "Storm & Gale."

The Paddock Club in Miami is owned by a Jewish mob guy named Silverstein. We're held over week after week. We do three shows a night and all the name guys like Joey Bishop, Jan Murray, and Red Buttons, who are working the big clubs, come at two in the morning to watch these two kids doing burlesque sketches. They ask us, "Where the hell do you get this stuff?" and we tell them, "From our fathers." They can't get over it.

Lou and I love Dinah Washington and there's a bar across the street from the Paddock in the Flamingo Hotel that has a jukebox. We put a dollar's worth of nickels in it to keep playing Dinah Washington records over and over again. We're sipping on our sodas and this tough guy named Blackie comes over and pulls the plug out of the jukebox. I ask him, "What are you doing?" Blackie says, "I don't want to listen to that fuckin' music." I tell him, "Hey, we put our money into it," and we get into an argument. I ask, "You wanna walk outside?" and he says, "I don't have to walk outside. I know where you work. I want to see what a tough guy you are when I've got you on your knees and I'm holding a gun to your head. What are you gonna do then?" I tell him, "I'll stick the gun up your ass."

Lou and I panic. We get a bat and we keep it onstage. We're doing our act and watching everybody coming into the club, waiting for Blackie. The show ends and in walks a guy named Lou Farber, who's an ex-bantamweight fighter from my old neighborhood who knows my father. He's working as a masseur in one of the hotels. Farber comes over and says, "I hear you had a problem. What happened?" So I tell him this guy, Blackie, is going to see how tough I am when I'm on my knees with a gun to my head. He asks if I know where he hangs out. I tell him, "Yeah, across the street in the hotel. He plays cards in the lobby all the time." He says, "Let's go."

We can see guys playing cards in a room off the hotel lobby. Farber says, "Is he any of those?" I say, "Yeah, that guy sitting at the head of the table. Blackie." He walks over to Blackie and he says, "Hey you. I wanna talk to you." Blackie says, "I'm busy." Farber says, "I don't give a fuck what you are, I wanna talk to you now." Blackie realizes this is the real thing, so he gets up and they walk into the lobby. He tells Blackie, "I hear you threatened this kid. You're going to put a gun to his head." Blackie says, "I was just kiddin'." Farber says, "You're kidding? You tell a kid like this that you're gonna put a gun to his head? Let me tell you something: From now on, your life's work is to be sure nobody hurts this kid. If he so much as trips and hurts himself, I'll come lookin' for you and you better have your gun. And another thing: I bet if I let the kid fight you, he'd beat you." I say, "Yeah, I'll fight him!" and Farber says, "Shut the fuck up!" But the problem has been dealt with.

Lou gets drafted around 1951 during the Korean War, so that's the end of Storm & Gale. Technically speaking, I'm drafted before Lou, but I'm stamped 4-F because I had that *other* kind of "chorea" when I was twelve. They look at my records and they don't know if I could have a relapse or not. They're concerned that if I start twitching while I'm holding a rifle, I'm not a guy you want to be around, so they decide I shouldn't be in the army, and that's that.

CHAPTER NINE

After Lou is drafted, I develop an act on my own and I keep the name Storm, because that's how everybody knows me. My father doesn't think I'm funny, so when Lou goes into the service, he asks, "What are you going to do now?" I tell him, "I'm gonna do a single." He says, "You're a monologist? Who do you think you are? Jan Murray?" He's concerned that I won't make it. His attitude is – and this is the vaudeville side of him – "If you're gonna do that, you have to have a specialty to fall back on." In vaudeville, a comic also sings and dances, like Bob Hope, or he plays an instrument. It's a safety valve, if the jokes aren't working. I know a lot of comics that play instruments – not well, but they play them. So if your material isn't going over, you can do "When the Saints Go Marching In" on trumpet and get applause and go off to at least a comfortable feeling. But to me, that isn't the answer. To me, those are copouts.

So I go out and start doing a single and it's a real struggle. It's tough. I do a joke about a guy chasing his girlfriend: "Where are you?" No answer. "Where are you?" No answer. "Where are you? I'll find you and rape you!" "I'm hiding in the closet." They love it, but when I think about it now, it's a terrible, tasteless joke. I do a piece that another comic gave me, a very talented guy named Georgie Hopkins. It's called "The Blind Date." I ask the audience, "Any blind dates here tonight?" On blind dates, the girls get up and go into the ladies room and talk about the guys, so I talk about what they're saying about him – little jokes and things. At the end of it, I say, "So girls," and I sing, "Don't give him a kiss to build a dream on, or his imagination will make the dream come true." I do jokes and I fill a half-hour with a lot of nothing, but at least I have an act.

I do "The Blind Date" at a club called The Stagecoach in Jersey and one night, Phil Foster is in the audience. After a particularly good performance, I go over to Phil, expecting him to tell me what a great job I did. Instead, he tells me, "Either you're very stupid or you got a lot of nerve." I ask him why and he says, "You just did seven minutes of my act! That 'Blind Date' bit is mine!" I tell him, "Phil, if I knew it was yours, I'd never do it in front of you. I got the piece from Georgie Hopkins!" He softens and says, "Forget it. Everybody steals from me, so go ahead and use it."

I work with a colorful Greek agent named Nico Kavera, who has an elaborate code set up to save money on long-distance calls. He makes a person-to-person collect call to "Mr. Howard Storm" and I tell the operator, "Mr. Storm isn't here, but I can take a message." Nico tells the operator, "Have Mr. Storm call Nico Kavera in Daytona Beach at the Roosevelt Hotel." That means I'm working the Roosevelt lounge. "Tell him to call me at 3:00." That means the rehearsal time is 3:00. Now he's going to tell me how much I'm going to be paid: "Tell him to call me in room 175." I say, "Operator, ask him if I can call him in room *200*." "Tell him he's lucky he's in room 175!" and he slams the phone down. But hey – it was a free call.

All the comics hang out at Hansen's Drugstore on 51st and 7th Avenue to swap stories and find out what kind of jobs are available. Unless you're making seven-fifty or a thousand dollars a week, you can't get an agent. At the time, the only talent agencies are GAC, William Morris and MCA, and they don't want to sign anyone who isn't already making good money. So we go around to all the little, independent agents to find out if there are any jobs. An agent says, "I got Saturday night for you," which means twenty-five bucks. You're hoping he has Friday and Saturday, which is fifty bucks. Better still is Friday, Saturday, Sunday, which comes to seventy-five bucks. So if he says he's got Saturday, you leave and try to find a better deal. By Wednesday, you start to get nervous that you're not going to find anything better, so you go running back to the first guy to see if the Saturday slot is still open. Most of the time, somebody panics *before* you and the job is no longer available.

After you make the rounds with all the small-time agents, you meet at Hansen's with all your friends. It's like the Schwab's of the New York standup world.

During the Korean War, another of my friends is drafted into the army, Sheldon Guralnik, so we have a going-away party. They all come out to Dave Harris' club in Bayside, Long Island, where I'm working. That night, I get heckled, so I handle the heckler in the usual way and then I come offstage. One of our guys, Tony DiBona, is *furious*. "Why'd you let that guy get in the middle of your act? Why didn't you go over with the mic and whack him in the head?" I tell him, "Tony, I handled it. That happens all the time. Don't worry about it." About twenty minutes later, Tony comes over and says, "Get the check. We gotta go." I ask, "Why?" "Get the check. We gotta go." I say, "Tony, will you tell me what happened?" He says, "Nothin'. I seen that guy that heckled you go into the bathroom, so I follow him in and I put his head in the toilet bowl. Get the check. We gotta go." So we get the check and we leave, but it costs me my whole salary, because I get twenty-five bucks for the night, but we don't have enough money for the check. I have to throw in my twenty-five to cover it.

An agent, Irving Charnoff, books me at a club in Johnston, Rhode Island, right on the edge of Providence. It's called the El Morocco and it's owned by two brothers, Gino and Irish. I'm there for three days and I'm doing very well, then Gino comes over and tells me, "You got a phone call in the kitchen." I go into the kitchen and he hands me the phone. It's Irving. He says, "Howard, they like you very much. They're very happy with you. But...they...they have a comedian who is a local who does a lot of business and they want to bring him in for the weekend, so I...I'll book you up in Maine for the rest of this week." I tell him, "No, Irv, I'm not going to Maine. I've been here for three days. Tell 'em if they want this other guy to pay me off." It's 175 bucks. I say, "Pay me off and that'll be it." Irving says, "Well, okay, I...I'll talk to them. Put 'em back on." I say, "Gino, he wants to talk to you." I hear Gino: "Okay, Irving. He stays. Fine." Gino hangs up, turns to me and says, "Every night when you go out to your car, look over your shoulder." Great.

There's a young couple at the El Morocco, Bobby Day and Babs – a husband and wife dance team. I tell them, "Do me a favor before we go out. Give me your tap shoes." I take their tap shoes that have big wooden blocks inside and I put them in shoe bags and hang them over my wrists like nunchucks. I go outside and walk over to the wrong car on purpose, then look around to make sure nobody is there. The dancers stand in the doorway and then I tell them, "Okay." We jump in my car and I drive back to the hotel and give them back their shoes.

Next night, Irish comes into the little dressing room and says, "Listen, you little prick. I'm not my brother." I tell him, "I know you're not. You're twice as dumb and twice as fat." I'm against the wall, being held by the throat, and he's about to punch my head in. I tell him, "Before you do that, let me tell you that if you hit me, I'll own this club." He says, "What are you, a fuckin' New York lawyer?" I say, "Yeah." "New York Jew lawyer" is the implication. He backs off.

It's Sunday night, the late show, and nobody's there. They announce that everybody can go home "*except* the comic." The band, everybody is dismissed, but I have to go on. I'm waiting and all of a sudden four guys come in with fedoras, sit down at a table, and I have to do my act. I walk out and I start to talk about what they're thinking. I say, "He's a small guy. What does he weigh, 130 pounds maybe? He's a little Jew comic. I could beat the shit out of him. But maybe he knows how to fight. Maybe we should go two guys at him. But if he's *really* good, maybe we need three." They start to laugh and one guy turns to Gino and says, "Hey, Gino. What are you tellin' us this kid's not funny? He's funny. Hey, kid! Come here! Sit down!" One guy asks me, "You want me to talk to Gino? Ask him to keep you another week?" I tell him, "No, no thank you. I want outta here!"

And that's that for the El Morocco.

This brings us to The Copa in Youngstown, Ohio and the cliff-hanging incident in the beginning of this book. As you recall, the owner is a tough guy named Shaky Naples. Shaky's bodyguard, Big Ralph, likes to kid around by sticking a gun in my face. One night, Big Ralph and Shaky's brother, Billy, try to stick me up and then march me down to Shaky's office, where they open a desk drawer and show me a .38 special pistol, which I pick up and hold on the two of them. I tell them to put their hands on their heads and not to make a move for the door or "I'll put a bullet in your ass," but I really have no idea what the hell I'm doing or where this is going.

Suddenly, in walks Shaky, who sees me holding a gun on his brother and his bodyguard! He says, "What the fuck is goin' on here?!" I tell him, "This asshole keeps sticking a gun in my face. Now he knows what it feels like to have a gun pointed at him." Shaky asks Ralph, "You pullin' a *gun* on the kid?" Ralph says, "Hey, we were just kiddin' around." Shaky slaps him in the face and says, "From now on, you take care of this kid and you make sure nobody bothers him." The rest of the week, I have to have lunch *and* dinner with these assholes, because Shaky tells them to do it.

That's not the only close call I have at The Copa. Another night, I'm onstage telling jokes and a guy goes running through the room. There's fear in his eyes like I've never seen. He runs through the door and into the kitchen, towards the parking lot. There's another guy coming after him who's very calm and very well dressed. He's wearing a black suit, a black fedora, and a matching gun. I see the gun and I start to tell the jokes faster. Then he *fires*. I dive off the stage, scurry into the kitchen and there's Shaky Naples. Frantic, I tell him, "Shaky! There's a guy out there with a gun and he's *shooting!*" Shaky asks, "Hey, is he shootin' at *you?*" I say, "No." He says, "Then get out there and finish your act!"

Shaky's quite a character. Eventually, he gets blown up in a Cadillac.

One time, comedian Norm Crosby and I are standing in front of the Tremont Hotel in Boston and he introduces me to a guy named Big Leo, who asks me, "Where you workin, kid?" I tell him, "I open Monday at The Frolic in Revere Beach," which is a mob-owned club about five miles north of Boston. He says, "Great! I'm comin' out there Thursday. A friend of mine's gettin' married and we're having a bachelor's party there." I say, "Okay, great."

I'm at The Frolic and I come out onstage. Four hundred guys are yelling across tables, talking to each other, some guys are standing, some are walking around. I'm trying to work and it's impossible. They have no interest in watching the show. Finally, Big Leo gets up and he yells, "Quiet!!" Boom! There's a hush. He turns to the crowd and says, "I know dis kid. He's a good kid. Next guy dat makes a sound, I'll knock him on his ass! You got that? *Quiet!!*" I do my entire act to silence. Finally, I finish and they play my music to take me off. Big Leo gets up. They all get up – and give me a standing ovation. I'm the only comic in the world who does his act and doesn't get one laugh – but gets a standing ovation.

Instead of leaving, the bachelor party sticks around and continues drinking and partying. After I leave the stage, I'm up in my dressing room thinking, "Oh, God! I gotta go out and do a *late* show for these people!" and I'm panicked. I only have one act, but the audience is staying put, so I've got to come up with fresh material. Whenever that happens, I do impressions and throw other stuff in so they won't have to sit through the same material twice. I'm up there wondering what the hell I'm going to do for my second show. Suddenly, I hear, "Carmine, if you ruin my brother's wedding, I'll *kill* ya!" Then I hear, "Tommy, put the gun away!" Next thing I know, chairs are flying and there's a riot going on. I turn to the girls in the chorus and I say, "I don't think we've got a second show." We leave the club, get in our cars, and off we go.

CHAPTER TEN

In 1954, I get a job at Banner Lodge in Moodus, Connecticut. It's much more erudite than the other clubs or the Catskills. It's younger, hipper people and it's a great job. Jack Banner is the owner, a lovely man and a first cousin of Zero Mostel who, at the time, can't get work in TV or movies because he's been blacklisted.

During the blacklist, nightclubs and the theatre are still available to performers, so Jack books Zero at the lodge as often as he can and pays him top dollar, because he knows Zero's in trouble. Zero works there a few times and I get friendly with him. During afternoon rehearsal, Zero is about to go on and he asks me, "Do you wanna do a number with me?" I say, "Okay." He says, "I'm gonna introduce you as America's foremost folk dancer and then we'll do a folk dance together." I ask, "What'll we do?" He tells me, "Just follow me. Do whatever I do." At lunch, he says, "Oh, one thing: No matter what happens, *don't laugh*." I say, "Okay." At dinner, he says, "Oh yeah, another thing: There'll be a moment where I'll go towards you and I'll veer off and you'll miss me. If you want to take a fall there, that's okay." I tell him, "Okay."

Zero introduces me, "Ladies and gentlemen, you may not know this about Howie Storm, but he's America's foremost folk dancer. We're gonna do a little dance for you – one of his favorites." I come out and Zero starts humming folk-dance music and he starts dancing. He goes around me and I go around him and then he veers off and I take a fall. I get up. He comes over to me and whispers, "Why'd you fall?" I say, "What do you mean why'd I fall? You *told* me to fall." He asks me, "Do you do anything anybody tells you, you moron?" We go on with the dance. He gets close and whispers, "How come you're not laughing?" I say, "'Cause you *told* me not to laugh." He asks, "Don't you think I'm funny?" He's messing with me. Typical Zero. Then he puts his nose up against mine and his head slips off. He licks his palm, wipes it on my nose, puts his nose there and it stays. He grabs me by the ass and I can't get my hands around his body! We're in profile and Zero's bouncing me with his big belly and the audience is hysterical. We finish it, we're backstage and he says, "You're a very disciplined actor. I'm very impressed." I say, "Thank you."

About a year goes by and I'm walking up 7th Avenue near the Latin Quarter. I see Zero walking towards me. I say, "Z!" Suddenly, he starts singing that same folk-dance song and coming towards me and we do the dance. People start crowding around. They don't know who *I* am, but they see it's Zero Mostel, so we get a big crowd. We do the entire dance, he finishes, he keeps going and I keep going. It's his way of telling me he remembers me from Banner Lodge.

I meet another interesting fellow when I'm working at Banner Lodge, but he isn't a comedian. He's a psychiatrist named Eddie Brownstein, a delightful, sweet guy who loves playing jazz piano. I tell him that I might want to go into therapy, because I'm very angry at my mother over all the beatings I'd taken. I also want to find out what's going on with me. I'm not progressing professionally the way I'd hoped – although I'm stubborn enough to hang in, because I'm going show my father that I can do it, dammit.

Eddie Brownstein tells me, "I can't take you on, because we're friends, but I'm gonna recommend a guy." He puts me in touch with Dr. Paul Bradlow, who is brilliant, just sensational. Through therapy, I gradually come to realize it isn't my mother I'm so angry with; it's my *father* who's the culprit, because he's always Mr. Nice Guy. But the truth is, he's completely irresponsible. My mother is left to handle disciplining us, keeping the family afloat, keeping us going. I slowly begin to comprehend the family dynamics and I'm eventually able to forgive them both. I come to understand why my father is the man he is. He has three sisters and a mother who dote on him, as does my mother, so he's just one of those guys that everybody takes care of.

In therapy, I'm always talking to Dr. Bradlow about how I tell someone a story about something that really happened to me and they say, "Oh that's funny! You do that in your act, right?" and I get annoyed when people ask me that. Over time, I begin to realize that

I *should* be doing stories like that in my act, instead of just standing there and telling jokes. I continue seeing Dr. Bradlow for a quite a few years, so the transformation in the style of my material is a long-term process, getting away from joke-joke-joke and getting more into talking about my actual experiences and observations. This will eventually pay off in a big way. In the meantime, however, I continue playing clubs and telling jokes.

I'm playing a club in Washington, D.C., opening for a very tall, very attractive, very talented singer named Marilynn Lovell. The club is owned by some Chinese people who are used to seeing tap dancers that tell a few jokes and musicians that do a little comedy. They can't figure out *what* I'm doing, just standing there talking. I hear them in the back of the club saying, "What he do? He just talk talk talk! No dance, no sing, nothing! Talk talk talk! What he do?" They hate me.

At the time, I'm seeing a voluptuous blonde actress and exotic dancer named Rita Grable, who later becomes Mrs. Jerry Vale. We work together a lot and we date for a while. She's in Washington playing the female lead in *Will Success Spoil Rock Hunter?* and she calls me to set up a date. She's going to meet me at the club. I'm sitting with Marilynn when Rita walks in with tits up to here. Marilynn spots her first and says, "Take a look at this!" I turn and see Rita. I tell Marilyn, "That's my date."

Marilynn goes back to New York and I stay in D.C. for a while, because my friend, comedian Dave Astor, has an apartment there. I get a telegram from Marilynn saying how much fun it was working with me. Dave says, "Hey, she digs you!" I tell him, "No, she's just being friendly." He says, "Schmuck, how many people have you opened for that sent you a *telegram*?" I call Marilynn and we start dating. One night, we go to a steakhouse and everybody is staring at us, because of the difference in height. I'm five-five and she's about six feet tall with heels. I get her coat from the cloakroom and I get up on a chair to put it around her shoulders. Everybody in the restaurant breaks up.

Later on, I write a routine about being with a tall woman: "We went to a formal dinner party and got a little drunk and then we went back to our apartment. I figured out that if we exchanged shoes, we'd be the same height, so I wore her heels and she wore my shoes. We started dancing and my heel got caught in the hem of her gown. I tripped and fell and sprained my back and I couldn't get up. Luckily, there was a doctor in our apartment building, so we called him and he came up and examined me. He said, 'It's a sprain. Just take this pill and put ice on it, and in the future, I suggest you get a pair of men's shoes – you know, like the kind your *wife's* wearing.'" That becomes part of my routine.

In 1958, I ask Marilynn to be my wife and then we leave for the West Coast to try our luck in Hollywood.

Marilynn and I arrive in L.A. and in no time at all, I'm broke. The only encouraging thing that happens is I get into Jeff Corey's acting class. I'd taken an acting class from Josh Shelley in New York, who writes me a letter to give to Jeff, because his class is always full with a waiting list. I meet with Jeff, I show him the letter, and I'm in the class, which is just a terrific experience.

Shelley also gives me Tony Curtis' phone number, saying, "Call him up. He's a great guy. Tell him I said hello. Have lunch with him or something." But once I'm out in L.A., I can't just call up Tony Curtis and say, "Hi, Josh Shelley said hello. You wanna have lunch?" so I never call him. Sometime later, I'm driving down Sunset Boulevard toward Fairfax. I'm in my beat-up old car and there's a beautiful convertible Rolls-Royce in the next lane being driven by a guy with a great haircut. We get to a red light, I pull up beside him, I look over and it's Tony Curtis! I yell over to him, "Josh Shelley says hello!" He says, "Oh, wow, how is Josh?" I say, "He's great." He says, "Did you just come from New York?" I say, "Yeah." He says, "Will you please tell him I said hello? He's a great guy." As the light changes, I say, "I'll be glad to, Mr. Poitier!" I see him in my rearview mirror, laughing his head off. *The Defiant Ones* is currently in theatres.

CHAPTER ELEVEN

In the late '50s, Lucille Ball runs a workshop at Desilu Productions in Hollywood called the Desilu Playhouse, which is supposed to be a springboard for young actors. Some people refer to it as Lucy's Follies. I think Desi Arnaz is trying to keep Lucy busy so he can be busy by himself. Three people at Desilu handle the auditions: Lucy, the director, and the assistant director, Paul Kent, who I become very friendly with. About a week after Marilynn has been accepted, I audition and the director must feel sorry for me, because I really don't know why I'm there – and I *never* get any attention from Lucy.

Desi Arnaz is going to open the wing of a hospital in Palm Springs and he asks Marilynn if she'll come and sing, so we agree to do that. We park our old, beat-up Ford on Gower and we meet Desi at his office around 11 a.m. Desi's chauffeur takes our bags, puts them in the limo, and we get in the car. He asks, "Mr. Storm, is everything comfortable? Is there anything I can get you?" I tell him, "No thank you." I'm sitting in the middle, Marilynn's on my left, Desi's on the right, and we're in a chauffeured limousine. I have *literally* one dollar in my pocket. Desi asks, "Would you like a drink?" Now I'm a big shot. I tell him, "Yeah, sure." He pours me a scotch out of the bar in the back of the car. Desi asks, "Cigar?" I say, "Yeah, sure." So I have a drink and a cigar and both of us are talking. Me and Des. We're old buddies. To the chauffeur, everything is "Mr. Storm" and "Mrs. Storm."

During our trip to Palm Springs, Desi tells me the story behind *I Love Lucy*. CBS doesn't want him for the show because of his accent, but Lucy won't do the show without him. Philip Morris is the sponsor and they don't want to pay Desi a lot, so they offer him low-ball money. He tells them, "Okay, I'll take the money you're offering me on one condition: That you sign over all the film to us. We own the film of the show." They look at him like, "What an idiot! What's he gonna do with that film?" But he has the sense to know that somewhere in the future, that film might be important. They say, "Fine" and so Desi and Lucy own all of the footage for *I Love Lucy.*

Desi tells me the film studios *hated* television. They're frightened to death of it. But the film studios own all the soundstages. He tells me, "We'd rent a stage and after two weeks of work, they'd say, 'We're doing a movie and we need the stage next week,' and you had to go running around to find another stage and move the set." He tells Lucy, "The only way we're gonna be able to do this is to own our own stages." He has a meeting at RKO and he asks the owner, "How much do you want for the studio?" The guy says, "Seven million dollars." Desi says, "Give me an hour." Desi goes to the Bank of America near RKO and he says, "I own all the film." He shows them the letter stating that he and Lucy own the footage. He tells them, "I want to borrow seven million dollars and I'll put up our own film as collateral." They do it. He calls Lucy and tells her, "Lucy, we just bought RKO!"

Desi is great. He's so smart and he's the kind of guy you want to have a beer with. He's my boss, he owns the studio, but we talk the same language. I ask him, "What does it feel like to own a studio that big?" He says, "You can only wear one suit at a time. If it all fell apart tomorrow, I'd start again. I came from a wealthy family. My father was the mayor of a town in Cuba, but we had to leave because of Batista. When we got to America, we had nothing." At sixteen, he's working at a pet shop cleaning the crap out of cages, so he really is just a regular guy.

We get to Palm Springs. The limo drops Desi off at his house on the ninth hole of the golf course and he tells the chauffeur, "Stay with Mr. and Mrs. Storm at the hotel. When they're ready to come, you'll drive them to the hotel." He owns the Indian Wells Hotel. We're getting dressed and Marilynn tears her stockings. I call the front desk and ask, "Is Mr. Arnaz's chauffeur out there?" They say, "Yes." I ask, "Could I talk to him, please?" He gets on the phone and I say, "Do me a favor and get a pair of black silk stockings and charge it to the room." I'm hoping Desi's going to pay for the room.

A half-hour later, there's a knock at the door. I open it and it's the bellhop with the stockings. I tip him with my one and only dollar and I tell Marilynn, "Chances are, Desi's gonna pick up the tab, 'cause he invited you to sing and it's his hotel. Let's you and I go to the hotel dining room and relax and have a bottle of wine. Screw it!" We go and do the show and I'm sitting there while they're auctioning off things. A set of golf clubs goes for thirty thousand, because it's for charity. Somebody buys a golf cart for seventy-five thousand. I'm looking at all this money going out and I literally don't have a penny in my pocket!

Desi tells me, "I won't be going back to L.A. with you tomorrow, but the chauffeur will pick you up at nine o'clock. He's gonna stop and pick up Phil Harris and drop him off in Burbank and then he'll drop you off." Next morning, the limo picks us up. The chauffeur asks, "Mr. Storm, are you comfortable? You need anything? Mrs. Storm?" We stop at Phil Harris' house. Harris gets in and Alice Faye is in the doorway, waving goodbye to him. He puts down a brown leather briefcase with gold lettering that says "ALICE FAYE." Now I'm excited. I speak to Desi Arnaz the whole way down and now I'm going spend an hour and a half talking to Phil Harris the whole way back. I'm in show business! I say, "Mr. Harris, I'm Howard Storm and this is my wife, Marilynn Lovell." He says, "Nice to see ya, kid. Zzzzzz." Out cold the whole way. We get to Burbank, he gets out, says, "Good luck," and off he goes.

The chauffeur drives us back to Desilu to get our car. We tell him, "You can stop here in front of the entrance on Gower." He says, "No, no, that's okay, Mr. Storm. I'll take you right to your car." I'm embarrassed, because we have this beat-up old Ford. Finally, I say, "It's that one over there." There's a red convertible in front of mine. He says, "The convertible?" I say, "No, the black one behind it." He's holding our bags, but he suddenly drops them on the pavement and says, "Good luck, kids," gets back in the limo and drives off. From "Mr. Storm" to "Good luck, kids." Suddenly, our coach turned back into a pumpkin.

Desi is a great guy, but I don't enjoy working with Lucy. Looking back as a director now, I realize that her idea of directing you is *acting out* what she does. I tell her, "If I could do what you do, I'd be a multi-millionaire. That's what *you* do. I can't do that." Lucy has no patience for me.

They bring in Carole Cook, who's "Mildred Cook" at the time. Lucy changes Mildred's name, because her favorite actress is Carole Lombard. I'm called to the office to run a sketch with her. Carole has done it on the road for months, so she's playing it full out. She doesn't have to read it. I'm reading it trying to get a sense of the thing.

Lucy says, "There's a joke there." I tell her, "I know, Lucy, I just have to get familiar with it." She says, "Okay, here's what I want you to do. When you get to the end of a joke, count to three and then do the next line." I tell her, "Lucy, what if the laugh lasts for six or what if there's no laugh at all? It's not television. If we're doing this onstage, it's gonna be live. Sometimes, a joke will work and sometimes it might not work, but I can't just stand there and count to three. That's great for television, because you can put in a laugh in post." She finds it outrageous that I would dare question her, but I know I'm right. After that, when she's putting sketches together and picking the people to do them, she never picks me. She tells me, "You're such an ingrate. You and your method bullshit."

The sketch Carole and I do is called "Upper Berth." It's about a couple being interviewed by Edward R. Murrow, who is played by Robert Osborne. All the couple does is drink beer and screw and they have about eleven kids. All the guy wants to do is jump her bones. I'm doing straight for Carole, setting her up.

I remember a vaudeville trick of my father's. I put the can of beer on the dressing-room table next to the light bulbs so it gets warm, then I shake it up and set it onstage. When you open it, the beer goes straight up. I tell Carole, "Lean over it like it's a water fountain." Well, we get *screams* with that sketch. Lucy comes to me begrudgingly and says, "I owe you an apology. You're the only one in the show that's consistent."

Years later, I tell Carole, "Maybe I'm crazy, but I don't think Lucille Ball had a sense of humor." She says, "No, you're not crazy. You're right. She didn't. I lived with the woman." She lived in Lucy's house and they became very close friends. She said Lucy never got the joke and was not good at repeating a joke.

Lucy has no real wit, but she's a *brilliant* physical comic. A clown. She's great at mugging and all that, but she's also being protected by Desi. He reads a bit and says, "No no. Lucy would never do that. Cut this out. Cut that out." Whenever he's on his way to watch us run scenes, Lucy becomes like a child: "Oh, Desi's coming! He's gonna be here!" He comes in and watches from the audience. We do the scene and he says, "Cut out the phone bit. You don't need to make the cross here. Just say the line and then go out the door. Come back in and do this." Boom boom boom. Suddenly, the whole piece comes together.

While we're at Desilu, Paul Kent discovers John Lewis Carlino, who writes a play called *The Brick and the Rose*, about a gang member who's a junkie. Paul and I tell Lucy we have this marvelous play that can use almost the entire cast of the Desilu Playhouse, but she won't go near it, because it's about a junkie. She wants light, nice and sweet, so we put together something a lot less controversial – *The Desilu Revue*.

We do *The Desilu Revue* for television and Lucy tells the cinematographer, "I want the whole cast lined up at the end of the show so I can stop and say each one's name and say thank you and good night." The cinematographer says, "But Lucy, they're all different heights. I'm gonna have to move the camera up and down each time and it's gonna look terrible." Lucy's walking around pouting like Jackie Cooper. Desi comes to the set and sees that she's upset. He asks, "Lucy, what's wrong?" She says, "I want to do this thing with the kids, saying goodbye to them and mentioning their names at the end, but he says they can't do it, 'cause the cameras will go up and down." Desi says, "What are you, kidding me? Put apple boxes down. You make everybody the same size." He turns to the cinematographer and says, "What do I pay you for?" Boom. Problem solved. Just like that. Desi's amazing.

Marilynn and I are in Hollywood, but I'm not happy. I go to the casting people at Desilu and I say, "Look, you produce a lot of different shows where a lot of people have bit parts – one line, two lines. You got twenty-one people in the Desilu Players that can do that. Why don't you use us?" So they start using us. I get a call from director John Peyser, who tells me, "I'd like you to do an episode of *The Untouchables.*" It takes place in a prison and I'm one of the convicts. It's wonderful working with Robert Stack. Leslie Nielsen and Ned Glass are in it, along with a wonderful actor named Peter Leeds.

Peter notices that when I'm running a scene with one of the actors, the actor overlaps me, so he takes me aside and says, "He's talking right on top of you so they won't use your closeups, 'cause they can't cut. It's too close. You gotta watch that he doesn't do that." Even though I really don't know what the hell I'm talking about, I go to the guy and tell him, "Listen, you're overlapping me and I'm tellin' you now, you keep doin' it and I'll overlap *you* and none of us will have a closeup. We'll both wind up in the master shot and that's it. So back off." He says, "I'm not overlapping you." I tell him, "Fine, then continue not to." And he stops. When *The Untouchables* airs, I'm in shock at how many closeups John gives me. Plenty of closeups, plenty of lines, but nothing comes of it. I don't get any more real parts after that, just one- and two-line roles. I get a lot of those – the cab driver with the wise-guy line or the pizza-delivery guy – because they know they can depend on me to get a laugh with the punchline. It's an important responsibility, but when you've only got one line, you don't see a lot of money.

The Desilu experience does afford me the opportunity of becoming a footnote in television history: I make two brief appearances on *The Ernie Kovacs Show.* The casting woman at Desilu does casting for Kovacs and she gets a bunch of us jobs as extras on his show. In one bit, he's conducting a choir and we're all dressed beautifully in tails. As the camera pulls back, nobody has on any shoes and socks. In the other bit, I'm a timpani player with a big symphony orchestra and my drum is filled with milk or eggnog or something that makes it look like the cover of a kettledrum. I get ready for my big solo and at just the right moment, I bring down the drumsticks, only to have them disappear into the milky liquid. I never get to talk with Kovacs, but I do make two brief appearances on his classic show.

Across the street from Desilu is a little bungalow where Lenny Bruce lives, so sometimes I hang out with him. He's just starting to break through. His mother, Sally Marr, is also there, married to a young hairdresser that I really like. Lenny's daughter Kitty is still in her crib. Everybody hangs out there.

I know about Lenny before I meet him, because Will Jordan is very friendly with him and is always talking about him. Lenny's success is almost an accident. He's working a strip joint in L.A., doing standard stuff. Lenny has been on *The Arthur Godfrey Show* and he wins doing impressions of famous actors. When he does an act with his wife, Honey, it's basically a song-and-dance to "Carolina In The Morning" with straw hats and canes and a little comedy. Nothing unique or remarkable.

No one is particularly interested in what he has to say, so he starts entertaining the band, doing schtick, telling stories that we do at parties – but not for an audience. Lenny faces the audience, but the material he's doing is so hip, only the band gets it. The band screams and then they tell friends and before you know it, audiences are coming in to see Lenny rather than the strippers. "There's this guy doin' stuff that nobody ever saw!" That's when he really takes off.

For a while, he's working with a black kid he does schtick off of, who also sings and plays guitar. Lenny teaches the kid a few Yiddish words. I'm doing a bit called "Leon Baker," which is a party piece. It comes from a real experience I have when I'm waiting to see an agent and a tap dancer named Lawrence is in the waiting room with me. There's a filing cabinet there and I get bored, so I open up a drawer, take a file out, and I say in a German accent, "So, ze name is Leon Baker, ja? You are a graduate of Yale Univerzity? A colonel in ze American army? Ve know *all* about you. You could've been a general mit uz, but no. Americans von't give you dat shot because you're black. Tell us how many troops come through and ve give you all ze vatermelon you vant." It's every racial cliché you can think of, but Lawrence is hysterical. At the end I say, "I hear you guys have big schvances. Can ve see it?" He takes out his cock and the guy says, "Corporal!" The corporal starts to give him head and he says, "Okay, I take over from here." The bit becomes very hot all over the party circuit. People beg me to do it. So Lenny is doing schtick with this black guy and he hears about my bit. Lenny asks me, "You wanna do the Leon Baker thing with our show?" For one reason or another, it never works out.

Bob Fosse's *Lenny* is a wonderful film and Dustin Hoffman is brilliant, but when Dustin does Lenny's standup act, there's something missing. He isn't Lenny. If you're a standup, you *know* where the laugh is, but if you're an *actor* doing standup, you have to *find* where the laugh is, and there are some actors that can't do that. They may be brilliant actors, but they can't play the humor. It takes about fifteen to twenty years for a comic to really hone his act. If he's lucky, maybe he can do it in five or ten years. So for an actor to have to do that in three weeks is rough. Standups work hard at it. They're out there every night, either failing or doing great. Each night is a new experience. The atmosphere changes. Every night you walk out on that stage, you are naked. You are all alone. There is no one to depend on. With a singer, at the end of a song, people applaud. It's automatic. With a comic, at the end of a joke, either they laugh because they think it's funny or they don't, and you've got to go on to the next joke.

Some nights I go to smile and my lips are so dry, they stick to my teeth. I reach for the mic and my hand is shaking and I can't wait to get off. To get to a place where you're a really good standup comic takes a long time. Nobody can just go out and do it. So to expect an actor to do a comic's material in a film or in a play is very difficult. It's like the old saying, "Dying is easy; comedy is hard." The only actor I know that's really able to "become" Lenny Bruce the standup comic is Cliff Gorman, who wins a Tony Award for *Lenny* in 1972.

After the Desilu Players runs its course. Marilynn and I return to New York and really struggle to make ends meet, living in a fifth-floor walkup on 85th near 2nd Avenue. I'm playing clubs and trying to get different projects going.

I write a comedy album with a writer-friend named Danny Davis. We call it "The First Black President" and we have some truly silly jokes in it. In one bit, the accountant says, "Mr. President, you've got fifty thousand dollars here for tap-dancing lessons. That's an awful lot of money. Who's teaching you?" The President says, "Bojangles." The accountant says, "Bojangles? He's dead!" The President says, "That's what makes him so expensive."

I'm looking for a classy guy to play the President. Our first choice is Bill Cosby, but that doesn't work out. I see Scoey Mitchell doing standup at a black club in Brooklyn and I like him. We put together a demo using Nipsey Russell, Slappy White and Scoey Mitchell.

Mercury Records is interested in putting out the album, but they want to use Timmie Rogers, who does that catchphrase "Oh *yeah!*" after everything he says. I tell them, "No, we need someone who's less black." I don't want "street." Mercury says, "If you don't go with Timmie Rogers, then we're not doing it." We tell them, "Okay," and we move on. Next thing I know, Mercury Records is doing a comedy album called "If I Were President" with Timmie Rogers! A lawyer tells me, "Unless they're actually doing material that you wrote, they have the right to do an album about that subject. If you still want to sue, wait until the album comes out and see if it's a hit. Otherwise, you're going to spend your money for nothing." In the end, nothing comes of the album – or our potential lawsuit.

To add insult to injury, I get word that Slappy White sold our demo to Chess Records for two hundred dollars, even though he has no right to sell it. I tell Nipsey, "I don't know what to do. I want to sue him." Nipsey says, "I'm a good friend of Slappy's, so it would be hard for me to take action against him, but if you subpoena me, I have no choice but to tell the truth." Nipsey's a straight-ahead guy and it's sweet of him to suggest that. Bottom line: Chess never puts the album out, so just like the Timmie Rogers situation, nothing comes of it.

On the home front, I sense something is wrong with my marriage and it turns out I'm right: Marilynn has been having an affair with Hal Gerson, the director from Desilu who is actually our best buddy at the time. He's a recovering alcoholic, thirty years her senior. I figure she gets involved with him because her father was an alcoholic and it feels familiar to her. After Desilu ends, he calls her every day. Their affair continues for quite some time. While I'm working weekend nightclubs, she's hanging out with Hal.

Marilynn is seeing a therapist and I'm still seeing Dr. Bradlow. Marilynn's therapist says, "If you want your marriage to work, you have to tell Howard about the affair and see where it goes." She does, and it's truly heartbreaking and terribly painful for me. She goes back to California to do *The Danny Kaye Show* and when she returns, she tells me she wants a divorce. I say, "Okay," but a lawyer friend of mine talks us out of doing it, saying, "There's no reason for you to do it now. You can go to Mexico anytime you want and get the divorce there."

Marilynn is very upset with that arrangement, but our friendship continues and we continue seeing each other, even though we start seeing other people. I'm going with a singer named Claiborne Cary. Dr. Bradlow says, "You have to cut this off with Marilynn and then you'll know if you really want to be with Claiborne or not." I call Marilynn and tell her I'm not going to see her anymore and she starts crying. I guess Marilynn and I want it both ways; we want to stay connected, but we want to see other people, and that just isn't working out.

I get a job in Germany, entertaining American troops at various army bases. Marilynn and I already know we're splitting up. On my way down the stairs of our apartment, she says, "Take care of yourself." I yell, "My life is falling apart and you're tellin' me to take care of myself? Are you fuckin' kidding me?" Finally, in 1963, I'm working with Wayne Newton in San Antonio and we aren't far from the Mexican border, so I go to a courthouse and I get the divorce. Marilynn is very unhappy about it, but it has to happen.

In 1981, she marries composer/arranger Peter Matz and moves to Los Angeles. We become friends again and have lunch once in a while. Years later, I'm with my wife, Patricia, who really likes Marilynn a lot. We have Thanksgiving dinners together and so on. When Peter dies, Marilynn begins to drink heavily and has also developed Multiple Sclerosis. Whenever she falls, I'm on the list of people to be called to help her out. Marilynn and I spend five years married to each other and we become good friends later in life, but hers is a rather sad ending.

CHAPTER TWELVE

I'm divorced and struggling career-wise, so I move in with my friend, Dave Astor, on West 72nd. He just split up with *his* wife, so we have that in common. After a while, Dave has to get rid of his apartment, so I find a place on 68th Street and he moves in with me. By the way, Dave is the first comedian to perform at the Improv. Before him, it's strictly singers and Broadway stars.

Richard Pryor comes over to our apartment and hangs out, because he loves watching Dave at the Improv. He tries out his material for us in the living room. I like him as a person and I'm impressed with him as a comic. He's very funny. At the time, he's just beginning to wean himself away from doing Bill Cosby and even though I love it, I'm not sure his material will work in the real world. Dave and I get Richie a job in the Catskill Mountains, which is ludicrous – having Richard Pryor work in the Catskill Mountains. They occasionally have black comics – Nipsey Russell and Slappy White – but mostly they have black singers who sing "My Yiddishe Mama" and the audience falls apart. Richie bombs, but we know he'll get at least a little money out of it. I think they pay him thirty-five bucks.

A few years later, Richie and I are doing *The Merv Griffin Show* together. He comes on wearing a black suit, a black shirt and a black tie. I've never seen him dress this way. I tell him, "Richard, you look like the black Mafia." He gets insulted and he makes a few fake jabs at me with his fist. Merv sees this and says, "What's goin' on here? Why don't you guys get up and really do this? Pantomime a fight?" So we do and Richie won't let me connect with him – even though we're faking it! In pantomime, I shoot a jab at him, but he won't acknowledge that I'm supposed to have hit him. He does it to me and I make a face like I'm hit, but he won't return the favor. He has to win every punch, so I let him win.

About four months later, I'm out in L.A. and Dave Astor is staying at the Sunset-Marquis. Richie comes to visit Dave and I'm hanging out when he walks in. I say, "Hey, Rich, how are ya?" and he turns his back on me and speaks to Dave. I say, "Richie, what's going on?" and he won't answer me.

About six months after that, I'm at the Improv in New York and he's at a table. I walk up and say, "Richie, if you're angry at me, why don't you tell me what you're angry at?" He says, "You're a racist." I say, "You know something? You can go fuck yourself. I'm a racist? Fuck you." And I walk away. This is all because of my "black Mafia" comment on *The Merv Griffin Show*!

Years later, when he's sick and in a wheelchair, I'm directing a Showtime special called *Women of the Night* about the comediennes at The Comedy Store. Richie is wheeled in and he says, "Hey, Howie." I go over and say, "Hello, Richie, how are you?" and that's the last time I see him.

One day, Rodney Dangerfield calls Dave and me and says, "Listen, can I come over for a couple of minutes? I wanna try something out." I say, "Sure." He comes over and says, "I'm doin' the Sullivan show. This is what I'm gonna do. Tell me what you think." He does his routine and I say, "Rodney, it's fine. It's what you do in your act. Just *do* it." Later, he tells me I was the only comic that ever encouraged him.

On Thanksgiving Day of 1963, I'm driving up Central Park West in my Volkswagen Beetle and I stop for a red light. To my left, I see two kids dragging an elderly lady who's on her knees, holding on to the strap of her purse. They get the bag away from her and they're running down 81st Street. The light changes and I don't know what possesses me, but I make a turn and I'm driving down 81st Street in hot pursuit of these guys with the purse.

I remember seeing some cops on television jumping a sidewalk in front of a guy who's trying to run away, so I get ahead of them and I turn the wheel and jump the sidewalk to block their escape. I jump out of the car and I say, "Gimme the purse!" The kid with the purse is up against the wall. He's holding it behind his back and kicking out at me, "I ain't got no purse! I ain't got no purse!" The other guy is standing there and he's got an umbrella. I know from high school that some guys sharpen the tips of umbrellas and use them as weapons to stab people. I realize how dumb I am, because I'm caught between them. I keep turning from one to the other, saying, "Gimme that purse!" The kid with the umbrella starts walking towards me. I tell him, "You take one more step, I'll take that umbrella and stick it so far up your ass, you'll have a hole in your head," and he freezes. Then I tell the other kid, "Gimme the purse!" He's still saying, "I ain't got no purse."

Suddenly, a young kid, about sixteen, comes running up behind him, yanks the purse out of his hand, and stands next to me with his hands on his hips, with the purse hanging down. I look over at him and I notice he's wearing a yarmulke. I start laughing at this ridiculous sight and I say, "Super Jew!" I can't stop laughing. We go back and give the lady her purse, then Super Jew and I drop her off at her son's apartment for Thanksgiving. The police show up and we drive around the neighborhood for a while, but we never do find those damn kids.

CHAPTER THIRTEEN

I refer to Billy Fields as my best friend, so I want to talk about that special friendship, because it's a relationship that I think very few people are fortunate enough to have. There's some kind of draw, a special connection we have that can't be easily explained. I even tell him, "Y'know something, Billy? If you were a woman, I'd marry you!" We're both Jewish guys – Billy's real last name is Feldman – from New York, although I come from the Lower East Side and Billy's from Washington Heights, around 193rd and Broadway. We become friends in the early '50s, when I'm about 20 and he's about 22 and fresh out of the Marines.

Even though this is during the Korean War, Billy never goes overseas; he stays stateside and entertains the troops as a singer. He's terrific. I remember going to see him at a club in New York. He auditions to replace Eddie Fisher at Grossinger's in the Catskills and Steve Lawrence is the other guy auditioning. Billy gets the job. That's how good he is. He's also the vocalist for Maynard Ferguson's band when they go on tour for several months. Billy appears on a TV show called *Chance of a Lifetime*, which is sort of like *Star Search*, where singers and entertainers perform and then a winner is chosen based on audience applause. Billy wins four weeks in a row. He gets a thousand dollars each time and the fourth time, he gets a booking at the Latin Quarter in New York.

Eventually, Billy begins to manage other performers, including such heavy-duty names as Neil Diamond, the Four Seasons and Whitney Houston. The trouble is, Billy's a heavy-duty gambler, so he loses money as fast as he earns it. One time, he wins $22,000 at a crap table in Puerto Rico. He walks into the Tin Angel in Greenwich Village and a bunch of his friends are having dinner there. Billy's carrying a shopping bag with him. He dumps the cash on the table and says, "Dinner's on me." I tell him, "Billy, give me ten thousand to hold on to, 'cause you're just gonna go through it.

I want you to have something." He says, "No, no, Bruz, I'm okay." He calls me "Bruz," which is short for "Brother." He goes to Vegas, blows the twenty-two thou – and leaves *owing them* seventy-five thousand.

Billy's very streetwise. Luckily for him, he's friends with a mob guy named Milt, who runs charters to Vegas out of New York and Puerto Rico. He's there when Billy wins at craps. Milt tells Billy, "That's an amazing thing at the crap table, to walk away with twenty-two thou. I'm having a big party at my penthouse. I'd like you to come." At the party, Milt introduces Billy to his pals saying, "This guy just won twenty-two thousand dollars shooting craps."

There are two young guys at the party. One of them says, "You're the guy that won the twenty-two thou? Oh man, we're sorry. We beat you for two hundred dollars." They stole his chips! While you're playing, these guys are great at waiting until you're distracted and then grabbing a $100 chip. The guys start to give Billy back the money, but he says, "No, no, man. That's what you do for a living. You took it, so the money's yours. That's fine."

Milt is very impressed by this. Billy tells Milt that he still owes seventy-five thousand in Vegas and he's paying it off two hundred a month. Milt asks Billy, "What hotel?" Billy tells him. Two or three days later, Milt comes back from Vegas and tells Billy, "Forget about it. It's over. You don't owe them a thing." That's it. Billy never hears from the hotel again.

One evening in the late sixties, Billy and I finish eating dinner at a restaurant on 9th and 54th called Ralph's. It's about 7:30 and still light out. People are walking along the street. Suddenly, two kids run in front of us and one kid stays behind us. One of them says, "Give us all your money." I tell him, "Go fuck yourself!" The other guy has his hand in his pocket, which you only see in movies. I don't believe he's really got a gun. The kid says, "You saw the gun, didn't you?" I tell him, "I didn't see a gun. I see him with his hand in his pocket." He turns his hand and shows me a little .22 pistol. I say, "Okay. You got the gun; you get the money."

I give him my money. Billy gives him his money. The other kid in front of us, who's wearing a loud plaid jacket, asks, "How much is there?" I tell him, "I don't know. Thirty-seven, thirty-eight bucks.

I'm not sure." He tells the guy with the gun, "Count it." I'm thinking, "He counts it, it's short, he doesn't like the idea, and he shoots me. If he starts counting it, I'm gonna stick my fingers in his eyes and we'll take our best shot." Luckily, the guy with the gun says, "We'll count it later." The guy in the plaid jacket tells Billy and me, "Walk towards 9th Avenue and don't turn around." The guy behind us tells us, "Walk towards 8th Avenue and don't turn around." I decide I'm going to "direct" the stickup. I tell the kid with the gun, "Wait a minute. You got the gun, so you're in charge, right?" He says, "Yeah, motherfucker!" I say, "That's fine. But he's telling us to go towards 9th and you're telling us to go towards 8th. You got the money, so just let us know what you want us to do and we'll walk away." He says, "Okay, motherfucker! Go into that building and don't come out for five minutes." I turn and start to walk towards the building, then I realize Billy isn't moving. I turn around and Billy's telling the guy with the gun, "I'll remember your face, you motherfucker. I'll find you and I'll fucking kill you." The guy pokes Billy in the stomach with the gun.

I grab Billy by the collar and I yank him away and I tell them, "He's cool! He's cool!" As soon as we go into the building, the guys split. We run out and I tell Billy, "Follow the guy with the plaid coat, 'cause he's easy to spot." We don't want to catch up with him, because he may have a gun, so we're hiding behind cars, following him, running across the street, stopping, watching, never taking our eyes off the plaid jacket. The guy goes into a big dance hall called The Cheetah. Billy says, "Let's go over to Jilly's and see if we can find somebody with a gun. We'll borrow it and go back and get 'em." We're going to go back to The Cheetah, put the gun to that guy's head and tell him, "Now give me all of *our* money and *your* money and take off all your clothes." We're going to leave him standing there buck naked.

We go to Jilly's. It's eight o'clock at night, but only the bartender is there. Billy says, "Nobody's here. Let's have a drink." I say, "Drink? We don't have any money!" Billy says, "I have money. I didn't give 'em all of it. Fuck 'em!" I've been cool through this whole incident. The bartender pours the drink. I reach out to pick it up and suddenly my hand starts shaking and spilling the drink: It finally sinks in what Billy and I just went through.

For three weeks, Billy walks that neighborhood, looking for the guys that stuck us up, but he never finds them. Just as well.

CHAPTER FOURTEEN

In 1964, I'm playing the Duplex, a club in the Village that's run by a wonderful woman named Jan Wallman. Everybody plays there. Woody Allen is breaking his act in, Dick Cavett, Joan Rivers, Rodney Dangerfield. I've been gradually revamping my act, putting in more of my own experiences and getting away from joke-joke-joke. I know I can never compete with guys like Pat Henry and Henny Youngman, who tell one-liners rapid-fire. I'm just not all that good at it and I'm a lot better at doing what feels right to me – talking about myself and my experiences growing up on the Lower East Side.

One night, I'm doing jokes about the guys in my old neighborhood. One of the jokes is, "It's hard being a comedian in my neighborhood, 'cause you say something funny and the wise guys say, 'Hey – What are you? A *comedian?*' I mean, how do you answer that?" I use that as a running gag throughout my act. After I finish, a tough bar owner named Nappy calls me over to his table. Those guys don't like you doing stuff about the neighborhood unless you really come from there. Nappy asks me, "Are you from downtown?" I say, "Yeah." He says, "Yeah? Where'd you live?" I tell him, "Henry Street." He says, "Yeah? What school'd you go to?" I tell him, "Seward." He says, "Yeah? How come I never seen you there?" A high school of three thousand kids. I tell him, "I don't know. How old are you?" Turns out he's my brother's age. I say, "Well, maybe you knew my brother, Eddie Sobel." He says, "That's your brother?! Marone! What a tough bastard! He didn't take shit from nobody! He's Jewish? I thought he was Italian. He has a heart like an Italian!" That night, dropping my brother's name gets me off the hook.

Jack Rollins, the legendary manager, shows up at the Duplex a lot because of Woody, so I get to know him. One day, Jack tells me, "I hear you're doing some interesting stuff. I'd like to come see it." I say, "Oh no no no, it's not ready." He says, "Well, let me come and maybe I can help." I tell him, "Okay." He sees what I'm doing and he invites me up to the Stage Deli that night. We sit around and talk and he tells me, "I'd like to work with you." I can't believe what I'm hearing. I'd talked about Jack Rollins in therapy, about this great manager who handles everybody, but I never said that I wanted him to *manage* me, because he has all these intellectuals – Woody, Cavett, Milt Kamen, Elaine May and Mike Nichols. I'm truly shocked, but I accept his invitation. When I go with Jack, I change my name from "Howie Storm" to "Howard Storm," because I figure "Howie" is too much like Jackie, Joey, Bobby; it sounds too much like a typical standup comic's name and I'm trying to go a little classier than that.

Even if I weren't a client, just knowing Jack is a pleasure. Everybody wants to be around this man. He's very special, as smart as can be, but without flaunting it. The first act he ever has is Harry Belafonte. He turns Belafonte's whole act around. At first, Harry's a sort of Billy Eckstine kind of singer. Then Jack says, "You're from the islands. Let's use that." That's when Belafonte goes calypso: the tight pants with the big buckle, shirt open, this handsome guy. Harry leaves Jack, and it's a horrible shock to him. When he finally gets past the shock of it all, his next act is Elaine May and Mike Nichols. After Nichols & May, it's Woody Allen and Dick Cavett and so on. He just has such great taste. He has that eye for talent.

Rodney Dangerfield is getting really hot and begs Jack to take him on as a client, but Jack turns him down. I ask Jack, "Why'd you turn him down? He's so hot and he's a wonderful comic." Jack says, "He's very talented, but no class." Even though Jack turns him down, Rodney starts begging Jack to take on Robert Klein. At first, Jack doesn't take to Klein's personality, but Buddy Morra, who's part of Rollins & Joffe, takes an interest in him. Buddy gets Jack to drive out to Jersey to see Klein, who does fantastically well, just kills the audience. Jack and Buddy are driving back to New York and Buddy says, "Well, what do you think?" Jack says, "Effective, but not winning." That's such a clear and perfect summation of where Klein is at with his material before Jack takes him on.

Jack's philosophy on comedians is that you have to have a point of view that gives you a sense of being special. Jack feels that's very

important and he works on that with you. Woody's point of view is
being Jewish and not being able to deal with things around him, like
his piece about being Jewish and not being handy around mechani-
cal things. It ends with him saying, "As I got off the elevator, I could
swear the elevator made an anti-Semitic remark." That's a point of
view; a sense of who he is and how he functions in life.

I take the subway down to the clubs in the Village and if something interesting happens, I get up and talk about it. I develop a
piece about the Catskills that Rollins thinks is hilarious – and it's
true. I say, "The owners of the hotels have speakers that they nailed
to the trees all over the place so they could announce what's going
on, but they never know how to use the microphone. So this is what
you hear: [sound of blowing air into the microphone followed by
loud tapping] 'The mic is on?' 'No, it's not on.' 'It's on. I just pushed
the button! Don't tell me it's not on! It's on!' You hear them arguing
all over the place through the speakers. Then you hear, 'Will Clarice
the chambermaid please bring toilet paper to the lake house!' and
it would bounce off the mountains: 'Toilet paper! Toilet paper...
toilet paper...' right up to the governor's mansion." Nobody ever
talks about those things, which is funny, because that stuff happens
at Catskills hotels almost every day. I think it's the perfect idea to
build a routine around.

Once I go with Jack Rollins and Charlie Joffe, my career really
starts to turn around. After all those years of dealing with tough
guys in strip joints and low-rent dives, I'm being booked into major
clubs. Jack brings people in to see me and they book me into their
clubs. No one turns me down. He brings Enrico Banducci in and
Banducci books me for the hungry i in San Francisco, which is very
prestigious. Woody works it, Nichols and May, Mort Sahl, Barbra Streisand, Cavett, Cosby, Godfrey Cambridge. Banducci falls
in love with me and I love him. He's a great character. I go into
the hungry i for two weeks and I stay eight. Mister Kelly's in Chicago is another big deal. I work there three times, with Jack Jones,
Mel Torme and a terrific singing impressionist named Marilyn
Michaels.

When I'm booked into New York's famed Copacabana in 1966,
I know I've *really* arrived. It's my opening night, Thursday night,

and it's frightening. I open for singer Petula Clark, who is major at that point. Sitting ringside are Jan Murray, Phil Foster, Joey Bishop, Joey Adams, Jack E. Leonard, Henny Youngman. Every name comic would come to the openings. My mother and father are also there that night. Never mind that of the $500 a week I'm getting to perform, I have to pay $140 for a room to change in at the adjacent Hotel 14. The point is: I'm playing the Copa!

I walk out and start in and I'm getting laughs. Then I hear, "Slow down, kid, slow down! You're doin' good, kid. Just slow down." I look over and Jack E. Leonard is sitting ringside, talking to me while I'm working, which is getting me crazy. I tell him, "Jack, I'm a little busy now. Can you wait eighteen minutes and I'll be back?" and I turn my back on him and start talking to the audience. Everybody breaks up. There's a famous Broadway columnist named Louis Sobol (different spelling; no relation) who gives me a really nice review. He says, "Young Howard Storm held his own with Jack E. Leonard heckling him."

I have another situation with Jack E. Leonard and this time, he doesn't talk to me for a year. I'm working a club called The Living Room on Second Avenue. The audience sits very wide on either side of the stage, but the rows of seats don't go back very far, like in a regular club or a theatre. I'm doing my act and suddenly, I hear laughs coming in the wrong places. I look over and Jack E. is standing there, entertaining a table. I say, "Ladies and gentlemen, that great comedian, Jack E. Leonard! Jack E., it's so nice to have you. I'm so pleased you came in. Why don't you have a seat?" He says, "Ah, that's okay, pal, I'm okay." I say, "No, Jack E., please sit down." He says, "Nah, it's okay." I say, "Jack E. sit down. You're tilting the room." The audience screams. Big laugh. Jack E. Leonard makes a beeline for the exit.

Later, I see him on the street and he turns his back on me. He doesn't talk to me for a year. Finally, he says, "You little *cocker*! Where do you get off using me for a pawn?" I say, "Jack E., I was fightin' for my life out there. I'm doin' my act; you're talkin' to a table. All you had to do was sit down. I was trying not to be rude. I gave you a nice introduction, I asked you to sit, you wouldn't sit, so I had to do something to stop it and I came up with that line." He thinks about it for a moment, then he says, "Well next time, know who your *friends* are!"

I have a similar experience with Buddy Hackett at a club in Cherry Hill, New Jersey. I'm opening for singer Rusty Draper and Buddy comes into the club while I'm onstage. Instead of sitting down, he casually strolls through all the tables, stopping to say hello to everybody. Of course, I lose the audience. It's deadly. I dress and go home and I'm so goddamn angry at Buddy Hackett.

About a year later, I'm working at The Duplex. I come offstage and Hackett is standing there. He says, "You know something? You got better." I say, "*You* didn't," and I walk away. This is the same guy who once said to me, "Your father was very nice to me. I was in the Navy. I was about eighteen or nineteen years old. I was in uniform and I came to a club in Brooklyn called The Club Bali and your father was the emcee and I asked if I could get on – and he put me on. Your father was very nice to me." But meanwhile, Buddy is not nice to *me*. He's a very strange guy.

Buddy and Louis Nye are good friends and years later, we'd meet at the Hamburger Hamlet in Westwood. It's Louis Nye, Pat Harrington, Sam Denoff, Harvey Korman and me, but Buddy joins us every once in a while. Buddy tells jokes and I tell jokes. Everybody breaks each other up and I think that's where Buddy finds a new respect for me. After that, we're fine.

Joan Rivers and I know each other from working at the Duplex and other Village spots. Right after Jack Rollins tells me he wants to work with me, I'm at the Duplex again and Joan asks me, "What's going on?" I tell her, "I'm now with Rollins and Joffe." Joan starts to cry, asking, "Why'd they take *you*? Why didn't they take *me*?" I feel so bad for her that I push Jack to take her on and I think I'm partly responsible for getting Jack and Charlie to represent her.

While we're both Rollins and Joffe clients, Joan and I write a movie together. Back when I was working the army bases in Germany, one of the British guys in the band had told me that if you have a Rolls-Royce and you scratch it or dent it, they won't just touch up the fender; they repaint the entire car, because they want it all to match perfectly. That's a big expense. I get an idea for a movie about a very wealthy British guy, a lord, with a big mansion and loads of people working for him. He and his chauffeur have a wonderful relationship and when he dies, he leaves his Rolls-Royce to the chauffeur in his will. The first day, the chauffeur drives it into town and some kid on a bicycle bumps into the car and scratches the fender. He brings the car to Rolls-Royce and they say, "We'll have to repaint the entire automobile. If you can't afford it, you shouldn't have a Rolls-Royce."

He gets angry and he decides to paint the Rolls-Royce the ugliest color he can think of. In his garage, he gets a big vat and he mixes paint and he throws strawberries in. He comes up with this ugly, nauseating shade of pink and then he paints the entire car that color. The title of the movie is *Color Me Ugly*. Every day, he parks his pink Rolls-Royce in front of the company. Rolls-Royce has a board meeting and one of the board members, an elderly woman, says, "We're too old-fashioned. We must begin to think outside of the box." She looks out the window and says, "Now *that's* the color of the car we should be making!" He makes a deal with them and, at the end of the film, they're mixing the paint in a big vat and the chauffeur puts a ladle in and says, "Hmm, needs more strawberries."

Joan and I write up a treatment for *Color Me Ugly* that's about thirty pages long. I go out to San Francisco to work the hungry i and I tell Joan to leave some copies at Jack's office and when I get back, we'll see if we can get the project off the ground. The movie is my idea, so we agree that I will have first billing: "Written by Howard Storm and Joan Rivers." I get back from San Francisco, I walk into Jack's office and there's a pile of scripts sitting on Jack's desk. I open the cover and it says, "Written by Joan Rivers and Howard Storm." At the bottom, it says, "Property of Rugby Productions," which is the name of the company Joan shares with her husband, Edgar Rosenberg. I call Edgar and I ask, "When did I start working for you? Am I on salary?" He says, "What are you talking about?" I tell him, "The script says 'Property of Rugby Productions.' That means I have nothing to do with it. So I'm just a writer that you hired? I own *fifty percent* of that and I intend to get it."

I know their lawyer, so I call him and I say, "Les, they put *their name* on it!" He starts to laugh, because he's been through this a hundred times. I tell him, "I own fifty percent of this project and

I want a letter, signed by both of them, saying that I own half the property." He says, "I'll take care of it." He draws up the letter and everybody signs it, then Joan says, "Don't let Jack try and sell the movie for us, 'cause he's not any good at that." I tell her, "Gee, I'd better call Woody and warn him!" Nothing ever happens with *Color Me Ugly*, but that's how I wrote a movie with Joan Rivers.

CHAPTER FIFTEEN

After my triumphant debut at the Copa, things suddenly and mysteriously go south. I don't know why, but even after great reviews, I can't get a job for more than six months. Jack can't figure it out either. Finally, Jack gets me the Concord Hotel in the Catskills on a Wednesday night for 175 bucks. It's February, it's snowing, and I drive up in my little '58 Volkswagen Beetle. I get there, I do the job, I'm driving back, it's still snowing, and my car dies. I get out of the car and I just go crazy. I go nuts. I stand in the middle of the snowy road screaming, "I AM NOT A LOSER! I AM NOT A LOSER!" I go down on my knees. It's madness. "I'M NOT A LOSER!" I keep screaming it. Somehow, by screaming, "I'm not a loser," I don't feel like a loser anymore! I call my brother and I tell him, "I need 500 bucks for car repair, rent and food." Eddie says, "Not a problem." My brother is always very good to me and my life starts to turn around.

Business begins to pick up again. I even return to the Copa. Inside that legendary club, the big shots, the real major mob guys, never sit ringside; it's always the soldiers, the wannabes. They have power and they have cash. When you work the Copa, each week, you give twenty bucks to George, the maitre d'. You say, "George, I got six friends coming in tonight. Will you be sure they get a good table?" and the twenty bucks takes care of that. Three steps up from the ringside tables there's a railing and more tables and *those* are the best seats, because you can see the show over everybody's head.

The Copa is owned by Frank Costello, Joe Adonis and Frank Erickson. It's weird when I see Costello at the club, because he looks just like my father! Frank Costello hires a tough guy named Jules Podell to run the Copa, which he does – with an iron fist. He stands in the kitchen and watches every tray go out. If he sees a little bit of mashed potatoes on the edge of a plate, he stops the waiter and snaps, "Clean that off!"

Podell hires a ventriloquist named Rickie Layne, who works with a dummy named Velvel. Layne is very funny and very good. He and Velvel do a lot of *Ed Sullivan Shows*. One night, Rickie and Velvel are waiting backstage, which, at the Copa, is the kitchen. He's bored, so he decides to have some fun with the waiters. He makes Velvel say, "Hey, you! Baldy! Why don't you put some food on that plate and bring it out? People are *hungry*, you moron! Yeah, *you*! The tall jerk! Take your thumb outta the soup before you bring it out!"

Suddenly, in walks Jules Podell and he's loaded. He's one of those guys that as soon as alcohol hits his system, Dr. Jekyll turns into Mr. Hyde. He sees Layne and Velvel goofing around and he asks, "What the hell's goin' on here?!" Velvel says, "Mind your own business, tough guy. No one's talkin' to you." With that, Podell backhands *the dummy*! Velvel's head flies off its shoulders, goes rolling along the kitchen floor, hits a wall and stops. Podell walks over to the dummy's head, leans down and says, "You talk to me like that again and I'll *kill* ya!"

I return to the Copa and I'm opening for Tony Bennett. The two couples sitting ringside are soldiers, wannabe gangsters. I reach for the mic and one guy says to me, "Hey! Don't *bother* us!" I say, "Don't *bother* you? I don't bother nobody! What are you, kiddin' me?" I turn to the band, "Do I ever bother you guys? I don't bother nobody!" The waiter walks by and I stop him, "Do I ever bother you?" I keep doing this "don't bother" bit. Everyone's laughing – except that guy. I know that unless I get him to laugh, I'm in trouble, so I keep going: "I never bothered nobody. You can ask my mother. She told me never to bother anybody." Finally, the guy gets uncomfortable because everybody else is laughing and he gives me a little forced smile. Then I know I'm okay, so I go into the rest of my act.

After the show, I'm invited to a table with British actor Nicol Williamson and a bartender friend of his. The bartender says, "I want you to meet the best fuckin' actor in the world, Nicol Williamson." I tell Nicol, "I know your work. You're great." We talk and he invites me to see him on Broadway in *Plaza Suite*, with Mike Nichols directing. Watching him is amazing. He does three different American characters and you would never know he's British. We go out to dinner, we become friends, and he tells me to call him if I'm ever in England. Sometime later, I go to London to do the Playboy Club and I do two television shows there. One is *Frost on Sunday*, an Ed Sullivan kind of show starring David Frost. While I'm in England, I hang out with Nicol and we have a great time.

Years later, he's doing his one-man show, *Barrymore*, at the Geffen Playhouse in Westwood. I go backstage to say hello. It's been twenty years since we've seen each other. As I walk into his dressing room, he says, "Ay! Don' *bother* us!" He remembers the bit and we laugh about it.

After I go with Rollins and Joffe, I start making appearances on talk shows, which leads to a very gratifying experience: Doing *The Merv Griffin Show* with my father. He's been out of the business for fifteen years and I tell Merv, "It would be nice to have my father come on and do a routine. We could do two generations of comedy." Merv says, "Wow – that's a great idea," so we bring my father on. It's his first time on television and he's solid; such a pro. He's about seventy at the time. For me, it's a kick and a half to perform those classic routines with my dad on national television.

Sylvia Syms is a jazz singer that Sinatra loves – as a performer, not romantically. In 1967, I'm working The Living Room again and I'm opening for Sylvia, who takes a liking to me. Judy Garland is a huge fan of Sylvia's and she's coming to see her. Sylvia tells her, "Judy, don't come just to see me. Come and see the comic. He's very good." Garland is seated ringside. I walk out and I see everybody making a fuss and whispering, so I ask Garland, "Would you mind standing up?" She stands and I tell the audience, "*Yes!* It's *Judy Garland! Okay? Now* can I do my act?" She breaks up. Then I ask, "Miss Garland, would you mind if I gave you a little constructive criticism?" She says, "No, not at all." I tell her, "Musically, you're wonderful, but you've got to learn to *connect* with the audience." This to a performer who could connect with an audience like nobody before or since. I continue: "Nobody *cares* about you. They just sit and stare. Make eye contact. Get that audience to *care* about you. Watch when I tell a joke. Watch how I look someone right in the eye. I'll show you..." Judy Garland screams with laughter.

After the show, we're talking backstage and Garland asks me, "Are you available to escort me to Jilly's?" I tell her, "Sure." She wants to go there because she has a crush on Bobby Cole, who plays piano and sings there. I go to pick her up at her hotel and her kids, Lorna and Joey Luft, are there. She tells Joey, "Fix Mr. Storm a drink. What would you like?" He's maybe ten or eleven. I say, "Just sparkling water." We leave and we get on the elevator. It stops on the floor below and some people get on, so Garland pulls her coat up over her head. We get off the elevator and I say, "What was that with the coat?" She says, "I didn't want them to recognize me." I tell her, "Well, you couldn't get more attention than you did by pulling your coat up over your head. Why don't you just wave a flag that says 'I'M NOT JUDY GARLAND!'?" She likes that I'm not intimidated by her.

We get to Jilly's and we're given The Sinatra Table in the back of the room near the kitchen. We're having Chinese food and two guys in suits and ties at the bar are staring at us. Garland says, "You see those two guys? They're hitmen. They're out to get me. When I left Freddie Fields, he put a contract out on me. I spoke to Bobby Kennedy about it and he said to contact the FBI." I tell her, "Judy, these are two guys from Jersey who are excited to see Judy Garland. There's nothing to worry about. No one's gonna *kill* you." Then I bite into the egg roll and I grab my throat and say, "J-Judy! D-Don't eat the egg roll!" and I fall on the floor. She breaks up.

A few months later, Garland's appearing at the Palace with Rodney Dangerfield opening for her. A day after opening night, I get a call from her assistant: "Where were you? Judy was upset. She expected you to be there." I say, "Really? No one invited me." She says, "Can you come tonight?" I tell her, "Yes." I'm sitting at the Palace and it's just amazing. She always opens by walking through the audience from the back of the house and up onto the stage. The audience knows her act better than she does. The orchestra starts playing a medley of "The Man That Got Away" that segues into "Swanee" and finally "Over the Rainbow." Everybody turns to look toward the back of the theatre. Nobody's there. The orchestra starts up again: "The Man That Got Away," "Swanee," "Over the Rainbow." All heads turn to the back of the place. Nobody's there. Forty-five minutes later, Garland enters. She walks down the aisle and everybody's touching her and saying, "I love you! I love you,

Judy! We all love you!" and she's saying, "I love you, too!" She gets to me and she says, "Thank you *so much* for coming!"

Garland does a terrific show. When she's doing her last number, the audience moves into the aisles carrying bouquets of flowers and they walk towards the stage. They're standing at the pit, throwing bouquets and trying to touch her. She's reaching over the footlights but there's a six-foot gap between the orchestra pit and the edge of the stage, so they're falling into the pit on top of the musicians! At one point, a guy's in a box seat and two guys are holding his ankles. As she's walking off the stage, she touches his hand while he's dangling by his feet. It's an unforgettable sight.

After the show, I go backstage and her entourage is fussing over her, tears streaming down their faces. One guy says, "Oh, Judy! Oh my *God*! You were just...There are no words! You were just so...*marvelous*!" I say, "You wanna know what's wrong with your act?" The guy whips around and glares at me. She says, "Yes." I tell her, "First of all, you sing *old* songs. 'Swanee'? Al Jolson sang that! You gotta learn some new songs! Can you learn 'Hello, Dolly'? You learn 'Hello, Dolly' and I can *guarantee* you the Concord in the Catskills." The guy says, "Who IS he?!" but Judy loves it.

CHAPTER SIXTEEN

I'm finally working the big clubs and doing national TV, but I still feel limited. When I see Woody Allen's act, I see a genius. When I think about my act, I think, "I'm *good*, but that's not enough." I'm looking at spending the rest of my life opening for a singer, but if I do that, I'll have to depend on them. If they like you, you open for them forever. I just don't have the personality to become somebody's court jester, always available at their beck and call.

I have no idea where the desire to direct comes from. Even being around all the cameras and equipment on *The Untouchables* doesn't inspire me to direct. If anything, it frightens me, because I'm not technical. I don't know anything about that stuff. Even if I don't have the knowledge, I guess I've always had the *instincts* of a director. Back at the Duplex, I notice singer Pat Finley finishing her act and running off at the end of her last song, then running back onstage for her bows. I tell her, "When you run off and then run back, it looks like you're afraid they're going to stop applauding. You're a lovely woman and a wonderful singer. Why don't you just walk off and walk back at a nice, normal pace, rather than running? It's more dignified. Don't rush it." She tries it and it works like a charm. Somewhere in the back of my head, a director is hiding. Learning to direct will save my career and my life. That's where *everything* will come from. The real money and the real success will come from directing.

In 1968, I ask Jack Rollins and Charlie Joffe to get me a job on a film from day one to the last day. That film turns out to be Woody Allen's *Take The Money and Run*. Woody has never directed, so I figure there will be people helping him along the way. All I have to do is stand next to him, keep my eyes and ears open, and learn. I know what I want to accomplish there. I have a book with every shot in the film: What lens is used, what the distance is, how many people are in the shot, and so on. Ralph Rosenblum, the editor, is on the set with him a lot of the time and he tells Woody, "That's a real nice shot. Now give me an insert of his hand reaching for the glass." I write it all down in my notebook and that's how I learn all those little tricks.

I get $400 a week plus $40 a day for expenses, which is fine with me. I'm on the set, I'm eating there, I'm saving up some money and I'm learning. My official job is to run the scene for Woody. If I do something he likes, he can use it or not. It's like a stand-in, but we call it an act-in. I play Woody in the scene and then, when the cameras roll, Woody steps in. The cameraman says, "Good for me, Woody!" The sound guy says, "Good for sound, Woody!" Woody looks at me and I shake my head. He asks, "What?" I tell him, "I think you should do it once more. Something's missing."

After a while, Woody has enough trust in me that he says, "We're doing the breakfast scene tomorrow, if you want to think of some jokes or gags." I go home and write eight to ten things and give it to him. Some he uses, some he doesn't. In the breakfast scene, it's the honeymoon morning and Janet Margolin's a terrible cook. She pours him coffee and I have him pull a teabag out of the cup. I also suggest that she make him steak and eggs and the cardboard package with the steak is all burnt. I come up with another idea, but we can't use it, because it's too late. I say, "Woody, supposing you cut the steak and the first piece of meat you give to the dog and the dog rolls over and dies?" We'd have to get a dog trainer and all that and we're already on the set, so we can't do it.

Woody allows me in the editing room, so I learn a lot there, too. As the famous bank-robbery scene is originally written, two gangs of robbers are planning to pull off the robbery and it intercuts between the two gangs as they prepare for the heist. Woody tells me, "Pick any of the parts in the two gangs of bank robbers." I take a part in the second gang, not in Woody's gang. I'm the second to the leader and I have a bunch of lines. But when we watch that scene in the editing room, it's obvious that the joke is given away seeing both gangs preparing for the robbery ahead of time, instead of the other gang suddenly appearing out of nowhere. So now, all you see of me is I'm wearing a fedora with sunglasses and I throw a bag of money. Charlie Joffe has a bigger part than I do! He comes into the bank and says, "What's going on here?" I do appear in a later scene – wearing the same sunglasses and fedora – when Woody and his new gang blow open a bank vault and find a family of gypsies living inside.

We shoot for two weeks in San Quentin. Every morning, we come into the prison around seven o'clock and the warden gathers us all together and gives us the same speech: "If you are taken hostage, we cannot be responsible for you." I look at Woody and I see the blood drain from his face. The warden continues: "When you leave the group, make sure you leave with one other person and a prison guard. Remember, if you're taken hostage, we cannot be responsible for you."

One day, we break for lunch. Woody and I are walking together and there's a prison guard with us, so we're feeling safe. I look over at our prison guard and I notice that the patch on his sleeve says "RAHWAY STATE PRISON – NEW JERSEY." I know we're in trouble, because we're at San Quentin! I tell Woody, "This guy is not a real guard. He's an extra." Woody says, "Y-You're kidding!" I tell him, "Look at the patch on his sleeve. It's Rahway, New Jersey!" Woody, frantic, turns to the extra and says, "Act like a *guard*! Act like a *guard*!"

There's another incident where my familiarity with tough guys comes in handy. About a year earlier, I'm working Mister Kelly's in Chicago. An older guy comes in and introduces himself, then buys me a drink. He says, "They call me Papa Joe. I run a group called Seven Steps. It's for cons and ex-cons who are ready to come out of prison. Ex-cons who have businesses hire them." He asks me if I'd be willing to do some shows for the prisoners at Leavenworth and Kansas State Prison, adding, "We don't have any money, but we can pay your expenses." Fine. I go to the prisons, I do the shows and the audiences are thrilled to have any kind of entertainment. Back at San Quentin, some of the prisoners are standing around and I ask them if they know Papa Joe. They say, "Yeah, how do you know Papa Joe?" I tell them, "I did a couple of shows for him at Leavenworth and Kansas State Prison."

This is 1968, the height of the hippie era, so a lot of the young grips that are working with us have hair down to their shoulders and tie-dyed T-shirts. Every time we walk into the prison, we hear loud kissing noises and, "Say, mama! Hey, baby! Shake that ass!" screaming through the whole place. It's an eerie and terrible feeling. We get to a spot where the prisoners are going to do a scene. They see me and yell, "Hey! That's Papa Joe's man! He's okay! He's our man!" Woody says, "Where do you know these *people* from? The man knows *felons!*" He can't get over it.

We shoot a riot scene and Woody wants to use real prisoners as extras. We set it up, we explain what we want, and we do a rehearsal. Well, these guys don't know from rehearsals. They're beating the shit out of each other. There's one black guy, must've been about six feet tall, 180 pounds. I'm watching him and I can see he knows what he's doing. Bang! He hits a guy. Bang! He hits another guy. Everybody he hits goes down. He's catching punches and they're just killing each other. Woody says, "They're *hitting!* Why are they *hitting?* This is just a *rehearsal.*" He figured they'd fake it or push each other; just make a lot of noise. I tell the guys, "Listen, hold back. You don't have to do that. But if you insist on it, at least do it when the camera's rolling."

I ask the guy that's been knocking everybody down, "Were you a professional fighter?" He says, "Everybody in here is a professional fighter. We gonna do this again?" I say, "Yeah." He tells me, "Well, I wanna fight *you!*" The prisoners and the crew start laughing. I tell him, "You wanna fight me? Are you out of your mind? I got a left hand that's dynamite! I hit you on the chin, I'll put you to sleep for a week." He says, "Let me tell you something, young man. I punch so fast, I stop and watch half the fights I'm in!" A truly brilliant way to phrase it.

For all the hard work that goes into filming the prison riot, that sequence ends up on the cutting-room floor, although photos and lobby cards from *Take the Money and Run* still feature this deleted scene.

We have a wonderful camera operator named Til Gabani, a great old Italian guy who I latch onto, because I sense that he's "the guy." I stand next to him and talk to him constantly. When we finish a scene, we hear "Good for sound, Woody...Good for lights, Woody," but nothing from Til. Woody asks, "Til?" He leans out of his camera with a cigar butt jammed into his mouth and says, "If I don't have it, you'll hear from me, Woody." Woody likes that, so he calls out to Til just to hear him say, "If I don't have it, you'll hear from me, Woody." Every day, every shot. Til is efficient at what he does and very sure of himself, without ever being cocky.

One time, Woody asks for something and the cinematographer says, "You can't do it because of this or that." Til tells me, "You're Woody's friend. Tell him it can be done, that shot he asked for," then Til explains how to go about getting the shot. When Woody tries to stick up the Brink's truck, he runs down an alley, makes a right turn and there's a wall; there's no place to go. Til designs a slant board to lean against and he adds handles to it. Til stands on it with the camera and Woody runs towards him, and when he gets to the turn, he goes down and then comes up and there is Woody running towards the wall. It's brilliant. Til is a real problem-solver, just like Desi Arnaz with those apple boxes.

One day, Til asks me, "You want to direct?" I say, "Yeah." He tells me, "I'm gonna give you some advice. Hire a cinematographer. Tell him you want a particular shot. If he says he can't do it, fire him. Get the next guy. Tell him the same thing. If he says he can't do it, fire him. The first guy that says he'll *try*, keep."

It's a life's lesson, really.

Even though I'm looking to become a director, I'm still doing standup. I'm shooting *Take the Money and Run* during the day and playing the Playboy Club in San Francisco at night *and* I'm also doubling into the hungry i, because Mort Sahl gets into a fight with Banducci. Banducci calls me and says, "I need you to come tonight." I tell him, "When the audience comes in and they see me standing there instead of Mort, they're gonna throw things at me." He says, "No, no, don't worry about it." I tell him, "But I'm at the Playboy Club." He says, "We'll hold the show if we have to. Finish at the Playboy, then come down and do a show here." It's two blocks away, so I have to sprint from the Playboy Club to the hungry i. As it turns out, nobody is upset that they aren't seeing Mort Sahl that night. They come in, they're told I'm filling in for Mort, I do the show, and I don't remember a problem. I'm looking to get away from standup, but I realize I have a small following in San Francisco – the only city anyplace that I ever have a following.

I come back to New York after finishing *Take the Money and Run* and find an apartment through Milt Kamen at 17 W. 67th Street, just off Central Park. Marshall Brickman lives down below and Milt lives above me. Next door is an actress named Phoebe Dorin. One night, she says, "I'm having a little dinner party tonight and I'd like you to come." I tell her, "I'd love to, but I can't." I'm going to a screening at Charlie Joffe's apartment.

After the movie, I come home and I'm just about to open my door when I hear the party going on at Phoebe's. I knock on the door and I go in. There's Hank Bradford, a standup who later becomes the head writer for Johnny Carson. Phoebe thinks Hank will be a perfect fit for her recently divorced friend, Anita. I'm unaware that's Phoebe's plan, so I start talking with Anita and telling her my Judy Garland stories. The next day, Phoebe asks, "What did you think of Anita?" I say, "I liked her." She asks, "You want to call her?" I tell her, "No. I'll call her if you talk to her first and ask her if she's interested." Phoebe comes back and tells me, "She said she's interested." It's a lie. What Anita *really* tells Phoebe is, "I don't know if I can handle that ego."

Anita and I go out a couple of times and we realize there's really something there. At the time, I'm going with a knockout of a model in Chicago named Tonna Kay Handley, who was staying with me in San Francisco during *Take the Money and Run*. I'm going back to Chicago to work Mister Kelly's and Anita and I have gotten very involved, so I call Tonna to break it off, but when I get to the airport in Chicago, there's Tonna waiting for me. We grab a cab, go to my hotel, and immediately fall into bed, but that's the last time I see her. She doesn't fight the idea that I'm getting serious about Anita.

I have to go back out to California. While I'm there, Anita calls from New York and says, "I'm frightened. We haven't seen each other in two or three weeks. I don't know what's going on with us." I tell her I'll fly into New York for a week and then we'll make a decision about our future, but every time I bring up our relationship, she doesn't want to talk about it. On my last day in New York, she tells me, "I'll write you." I say, "I don't want a pen pal. If you're not out in L.A. by April 1, I'm moving on." That gives her about two months to make up her mind.

Anita shows up in L.A. at midnight on April 1 – just under the wire. We move into an apartment near Olympic and Canon. About six months later, she says, "Let's have a child." We have a big discussion about whether we should get married first or if we should have a child out of wedlock. As hip as we *think* we are, we're actually very traditional, so we get married in October of 1969. Our son, Anthony, is born on August 22, 1970, about ten or eleven months after our wedding. I've always believed in a family and I don't believe in having an only child, so I push for another child and our second son, Casey, is born on May 18, 1972, twenty-one months after Anthony.

My parents actually precede me in moving to L.A., because Eddie and his family move out here for business reasons. When I move to L.A., it makes for something of a family reunion – especially when Sylvia and her husband move to L.A. shortly after me. By the early '70s, all of the Sobels have shifted from the East Coast to the West Coast. This makes for some awkward familial moments. Anita and I are about to go on a trip and the doorbell rings about nine in the morning. Our housekeeper opens the door. I hear my mother's voice and then I fall back asleep. Next thing I know, I hear our bedroom door opening. I look over and I see her putting a little present on the nightstand next to Anita and then she leaves. I call her up and tell her, "Mom, you can't just walk into our house and into our bedroom. What if we were making love?" She says, "Why, I never saw that before?" I tell her, "Mom, from here on in, you're welcome to come over, but you call me." She says, "Oh, so I have to call to see my son?"

CHAPTER SEVENTEEN

While I'm out in L.A. playing clubs – and waiting for Anita to make up her mind about moving to the West Coast – I also take the occasional TV or movie role, just to keep money coming in. I do an episode of *Love American Style* with Bob Denver that has to do with a blind date and a hitchhiker. Then I do *The Governor and J.J.* with Dan Dailey and Julie Sommars, where I play an Italian butler who doesn't speak English. I have to learn it phonetically. There's a club in Santa Monica called The Horn that I work and the owner speaks Italian, so he helps me out with that.

I come up with an idea for a film about a standup comic, based on my life. The title is *Mother Wit*, which is a Southern expression for someone who has natural, innate wit. Ron Cohen, a friend of mine who was dating Marilynn after we divorced, goes to New York to try to make a deal, but it doesn't happen. Ron and his partner write a Western feature called *The Good Guys and The Bad Guys* and they hire me to do a role. We shoot it in Arizona and it's really a lot of fun. I meet Robert Mitchum and, for a while, I'm on his Christmas card list. He even sends me an album of him singing. He's actually pretty good.

One day, I get a phone call from a terrific young improvisational actor named Chris Ross. He's going to be in a movie directed by Jerry Paris and he asks, "Would you want to replace me in The Committee?" The Committee is a popular improvisational comedy troupe out of San Francisco. They're an offshoot of Second City, the difference being The Committee is a lot more political and they do a lot more social commentary than Second City.

It's nice of Chris to extend the invitation, but the truth is, he doesn't have the authority, so the director, Alan Myerson, says, "I'd like to see your act. Are you working anywhere?" I tell him, "Yeah, I'm at the Playboy on Sunset." He shows up with Rob Reiner, I finish my act and he invites me to join the group. After years of relying on prepared material, I start learning to improvise. It's really going out onstage balls naked. I'm with some terrific improvisers: Howard Hesseman, Gary Goodrow, Peter Bonerz, Carl Gottlieb, Dick Stahl, among others. I have a tough time at first, because they look down on me – a Catskill comic, that sort of thing. It takes quite awhile for me to be accepted.

Chris Ross is sensational, but he's a junkie and, in 1970, he overdoses at the age of 24. A tragic loss. The Committee performs at the Tiffany Theater on Sunset for two years, then we're invited to take over the San Francisco theater, because that group is going on a tour playing colleges. We don't have to worry about where to stay in San Francisco; we just take over the apartments of the members who are leaving. The problem is, I'm given John Brent's apartment. John is a brilliant guy. Unfortunately, like Chris Ross, John is a heroin addict and he shoots up. I get to his apartment, I go to lie down and I notice blood spots all over the wall. I look up and there are blood spots all over the ceiling. I get up, grab my bag, and go to a motel.

We work out of The Committee's San Francisco theater while their troupe is on tour, then we return to L.A. Our agent, Mike Medavoy, tells us ABC wants to do a one-hour show of improv each week. We sell them with a ten-minute sample reel that has a couple of pieces that we already had set, and then Howard Hesseman announces, "It's my great pleasure to introduce my friends, the Rolling Stones!" Howard is friendly with the Stones. He goes to London and they love him there. The Rolling Stones give us permission to use a cut of them performing on a TV show. After ABC sees *that*, they really want the show.

Cary Grant is on the board of directors of Faberge, the show's sponsor. Strange as it may seem, Cary Grant *loves* us. He comes to the Tiffany once a week, sits in the first row and screams; just hysterical. We encourage people to write graffiti on the front of the stage, on the walls, in the bathroom, anywhere. Someone writes above a urinal – and I still don't know what it means – "Ronald Reagan Fucks Corn Flakes!" We're talking to Cary Grant in the lobby after the show and he says, "You guys are just wonderful! You make me laugh so, it's just terrific!" He excuses himself to go to the john, then he comes out and he says, "Oh, that's hilarious! 'Ronald Reagan Fucks Corn Flakes!' I've got to call Ronnie and tell him about this!" It's unbelievable. *Cary Grant* is our biggest fan.

ABC sets up a photo session with Grant and The Committee. Lynn Lipton, part of our troupe, thinks everybody is kidding her. She pegs me as the most trustworthy of the group and says, "They all say Cary Grant's coming." I tell her, "He is." She says, "Oh come on." Grant enters and starts walking down the aisle. I tell Lynn, "You can ask him yourself if he's coming!" She turns and sees him and says, "Oh my God! Wait'll my mother hears about this!" Grant says, "Wait'll *my* mother hears about *this*!" He's just so charming and delightful. At the photographer's suggestion, Grant takes a seat onstage with the rest of us around him. The photographer asks, "Can you all move in a little closer?" so we block Cary Grant out of the picture entirely. He's hysterical. He loves it. Finally, ABC gets the photo they want.

In the ABC contract, we want the right to choose which members will do the show each week. There are about thirty of us, counting both the San Francisco and L.A. companies and we don't want one member to become "the star." So if, say, Howard Hesseman really scores one week, we don't want ABC to have the power to make him the permanent host. It's "The Committee." We're all equal and we all get paid the same amount of money. ABC doesn't like that, so they back off and then we walk away from it. Our TV series ends before it even begins.

The Committee gets booked into Caesar's Palace as the opening act for Blood, Sweat & Tears. We're told to be very careful about drugs, because the FBI has their eye on the rock group. They tell us, "Don't bring any pot or anything," but Anita bakes a gigantic pot brownie, which I put in a large manila envelope like it was my 8x10 glossies. Everybody is famished and grabbing handfuls of the giant brownie. We don't realize how potent it is. We're totally whacked at rehearsal.

Working Caesar's is like working a major theatre on Broadway, with grips and electricians and a whole crew backstage. Before we go out on opening night, they announce, "Committee, five minutes!" We all gather around and as a good-luck ritual, we do a hum before going out, like an "Om" mantra. When we come out of it, we see the grips laughing at us and our hippie ways. We do the show and we kill on opening night. The second night, we hear: "Committee, five minutes!" One of the grips says, "Wait a minute! They gotta *hum* first!"

When a show is *really* good, they ask you to do an extra show at two o'clock in the morning on Saturday to handle the overflow. This also gives the bartenders and all the performers in other hotels a chance to come and see the show. Caesar's asks us to do a late show. I remember Sammy Davis and Sidney Poitier sitting ringside for the two a.m. performance.

Caesar's gives us rooms, but they won't give us VIP cards for food, because Blood, Sweat & Tears has all of their musicians plus their entourage, so there are about thirty-five of their people. I gather The Committee members together and I tell them, "Listen, they're not gonna pay for our food, but there are seventeen guys in the band plus their girlfriends, their buddies and so on. They all get VIP cards, so they can sign off on meals. When you're in the restaurant, you're bound to see *someone* from that group. Let's go have a meeting with them." We go to Blood, Sweat & Tears and we say, "Listen, we don't have the right to eat as freebies, because Caesar's won't let us, but you guys all have VIP cards. If you see any of us eating, could you come over and pick up our check, and if we see you, can we give you our check?" They love it. They're all hippies: "Yeah, great, man! Beat the system! Stick it to the man!" They love it. Everybody is impressed that I come up with this idea. It works and we never have to pay for food. When Caesar's tells us, "We'd like you to do a two a.m. show," I tell them, "We don't have a problem with that, but since we're doing it for nothing, I think you should give us an extra day in the hotel." They say, "Fine." Everybody is grateful that I've swung another deal for them.

One morning after the band leaves the restaurant, we're having breakfast at about eleven o'clock and I tell Alan Myerson, "You want to see me get our check picked up?" He says, "Yeah." Dave Vickerson, the entertainment director for Caesar's, is having breakfast with another guy. I call the waitress over and I say, "Tell Mr. Vickerson that The Committee would like to buy him and his friend a drink." I know he's not going to want a drink at eleven o'clock in the morning and I know he's not going to let this little *pisher* top him. The waitress comes back and says, "Mr. Vickerson says it's a little early to drink, but thank you. It was a very sweet gesture." Alan says, "Ha! Mr. Big Shot's gonna get our check picked up, huh?" I tell Alan, "Wait; it's not over." We finish eating, we ask for the check, and the waitress says, "Mr. Vickerson picked it up."

The Committee asks me to start booking them. Basically, I set up the dates and fight for more money. I get us an afternoon TV shot that pays $7,500, then I speak to Alan about putting a company together in L.A. and going back into the Tiffany. That group includes Archie Hahn, Carl Gottlieb, Valerie Curtin and Peter Elbling. Dick Stahl's wife, Kathryn Ish, has never directed, but she wants to, so I tell her, "Okay, you got it." We go back into the Tiffany and I get ten percent off the top. We're there through the summer and it's a terrific experience all the way around.

The more I work with The Committee, the less I want to do traditional standup. Also, as the cliché goes, what I *really* want to do is direct. In 1970, I work a place on the way to Palm Springs and the audience is so rude and obnoxious that when I finish, I tell Anita, "That's it. I don't want to do this anymore." I'm still working at The Horn in Santa Monica. I go back there for what I know is going to be my last gig. The fact that I'm not going to be doing it anymore gives me a very liberating sense of "Who cares?" The audience isn't laughing and I tell them, "Y'know, this isn't new stuff. I've done this before and it gets laughs, so you're wrong and I'm right. I'll tell you what. I know you're not happy with me and I'm not particularly happy with you, so the next real laugh I get, I'll leave." I do a joke and they go, "Ha-ha-ha," sarcastically. I say, "No, no, no. You can't fake it. It's gotta be a *real* laugh." I keep working and working and finally, bang – I get them and it's a good, solid laugh. I tell them, "That's it," and I walk offstage. They're applauding and screaming, "Come back! Come back!" I walk back, I walk up to the mic and I say, "No, you had your chance," and I leave the stage.

This marks the end of my career as a standup comic.

*I'm about four years old here, posing on a
neighbor's stoop in New York, c. 1936. I think
somebody had just kissed me on both cheeks.*

The wedding of Abe Penn (whose father, Menke, was rubbed out by the mob) and his bride, Frances, c. 1936. That's me in the sailor suit on the lower left. Next to me, in the loud necktie, is my cousin, Dick. Above him is Grandma Mary Penn, then Abe & Frances, my father and my mother. Below my father is my brother, Eddie, with his arm around my cousin, Janice. Behind the bride – with the moustache – is Moe Penn, the famous hat maker. At the top, in the white tie, is Abe's brother, Harry. Above the groom and just to the left is my cousin, Bernice, who caused quite a scandal when she married black comedian Pigmeat Markham.

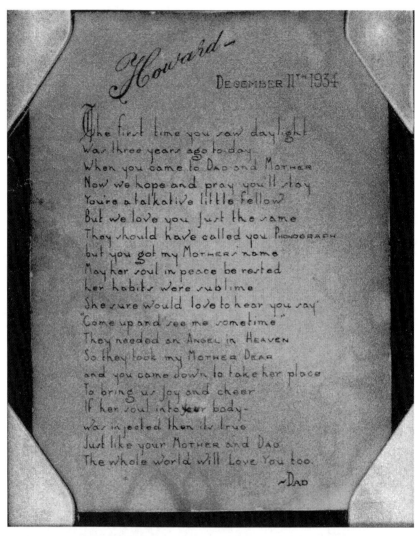

A wonderful poem my father wrote for my third birthday, hand-lettered by a friend of his – in prison.

*Storm & Gale: Lou Alexander and me when we were nineteen, at the
Beach Club in Daytona Beach, where we opened for singer June Christy.*

*During my standup
days as "Howie
Storm" in 1964. The
photographer kept
arguing that my nose
and forehead needed
to be retouched, so I
finally said, "Why
don't you just replace
it with a picture of
Robert Goulet?!"*

HOWIE STORM

My best friend, Billy Fields, and me in New York, c. 1969.

Making my Broadway debut in Fun City *(1972). Clockwise from Joan Rivers at the bottom: Joan Rivers, Renee Lippin, Gabe Dell, Noel Young, Louis Zorich, me, J.J. Barry, Pierre Epstein, Paul Ford, and Rose Marie. The show was a flop, but I had a blast.*

The great Garry Marshall and me in 1978 – the first season of Mork & Mindy.

The brilliant Robin Williams and me in 1978. His death was such a shock. There will never be another Robin.

The talented cast and crew of Mork & Mindy *in 1979. I'm sitting between stars Pam Dawber and Robin Williams (holding an egg). Reclining behind me is Conrad Janis. Above him is Exec Producer Bruce Johnson, with Tom Poston behind him. Garry Marshall is wearing his trademark cap.*

Tony Danza, Danny DeVito, Robin Williams and me (with my left-handed glove) at a Paramount/Garry Marshall softball game in 1979.

With the cast of Angie *(1979): Donna Pescow, me, Doris Roberts, Robert Hays, Diane Robin, Debralee Scott.*

The comedians table at the Carnegie Deli in Woody Allen's classic,
Broadway Danny Rose *(1984). From left: Sandy Baron, Will*
Jordan, Jack Rollins, me, Jackie Gayle, and Corbett Monica's back.

On the set of my feature film, Once Bitten *(1985), with Lauren*
Hutton, Cleavon Little, and twins Glen and Gary Mauro.

My mother and father on their 65th wedding anniversary in 1989.

Storm & Gale in 2017 – still a team.

Flanked by my terrific sons, Casey and Anthony, c. 1990.

Dancing at the Playboy Mansion with my wonderful wife, Patricia, c. 2005.

CHAPTER EIGHTEEN

I ask Jack Rollins and Charlie Joffe for another movie to work on after *Take the Money and Run*. In May of 1970, I take a break from The Committee and start in on *Bananas*, so I'm learning the craft of directing by watching Woody Allen work. We're shooting in a place called Bayamon, outside of San Juan in Puerto Rico. It's a tough town. A lot of fighters come out of there, including Hector Camacho. We're shooting next to a bar in the afternoon and there are a bunch of drunks out in front yelling and screwing up the shots. Fred Gallo, the Assistant Director, is yelling, "Silencio, por favor!" It doesn't do any good.

At two in the morning, we're going to shoot in a big field down the hill about six or seven blocks from where we were. It's a scene where Woody gets into a sleeping bag with a big, heavy Spanish guy. I always hang out with the grips and the extras, because they're my kind of people. We're ready to shoot the scene and one of the extras, a young guy, comes up to me and gives me a switchblade knife that's about a foot long when it's opened. He tells me, "Protect yourself. I hear them talking and they say they're gonna come beat up the gringos." I tell Fred Gallo, "This guy just gave me a knife and told me to protect myself, 'cause the guys from the bar are comin' to jump us."

Woody has a driver assigned to him who is an absolute stone killer. He's short with big, wide shoulders, a crew cut, and just cold as ice. Woody calls him "a mouth-breather." When Fred goes to have a meeting with the head of the Screen Extras Guild in San Juan, the guy pulls a gun on him and tells him what he wants. Fred goes back to Charlie Joffe and tells him what happened. Charlie makes some calls and they send a guy down from Florida. He tells Charlie, "Here's what you do. Invite this guy to lunch. Have a limo waiting in front of his office building, but make sure he gets in *before* you. I want him in the middle." The guy gets into the limo and bing! There's a gun in his ear. It's the guy from Florida, who tells him, "You pulled a gun on one of our people. Let me tell you something. You do that again and I can guarantee you I'll blow your fuckin' brains out. Now get outta the car." So that's why they assign this scary guy to be Woody's chauffeur and bodyguard.

When I tell Fred that these guys are coming down to attack us, he says, "Don't tell Woody." Woody never knows anything about this incident. Fred gathers all the heads of the departments together, tells them what's going on, and says, "Do not let Woody know." The prop guys are two tough Irish brothers from New York. The lead prop guy says, "Are you fuckin' kiddin' me? We're shootin' an army movie and they're gonna come here and beat up the gringos? Fuck 'em! Everybody line up! I got guns up the wazoo here!" He hands out .45s and M-1 rifles to everybody – real guns, but with blanks or "wads" as he calls them. He says, "Tommy, set the machine gun up on the truck." Then he tells us, "Okay, here's what youse do: The guy's walkin' towards you, just squeeze the trigger. If you hit him with a wad, he'll think he got shot. If you miss him, the sound will scare the hell out of him." Woody has no idea any of this is going on.

Suddenly, it turns into a bad B-movie: Headlights are coming down the hill. Three cars. The cars stop. Lights off. Motors off. Doors open. Doors slam. People bark orders in Spanish. They walk past Woody's Winnebago. We hear a loud thump and then the sound of a body hitting aluminum. Woody's bodyguard has hit one guy and knocked him into another Winnebago. We hear, "Why you hit him? He no do nothin'! Why you do that?" Then we hear, "Are youse guys actors? Do you have union cards? What are youse doin' here? If you don't have SAG cards, then pick up your friend and get the fuck outta here!" So they take the hint: Back in their cars. Doors slam. Motors on. Lights on. We finish the shot and we wrap in record time: twelve minutes. It's unheard of to wrap that fast, but we aren't taking any chances, in case those guys come back with reinforcements.

After *Bananas* wraps, I return to The Committee in L.A. In 1971, Alan Myerson says, "Anybody who wants to come back to San Francisco and work the theater there can do so." I speak to

Gary Goodrow, a wonderful improviser, and I ask him if he'd like to teach an improv class with me in L.A. He says, "Yes," so we start up a class and we wind up with twenty students. Gary and I get a lot out of teaching and, as with my advice to Pat Finley at the Duplex, my instincts for helping performers present themselves effectively onstage are fueling my desire to direct. In December of that year, however, I take a leave of absence, because Howard Storm is going to make his Big Broadway Debut.

There's a play called *Fun City* by writer Les Colodny. He can't get it off the ground, so he takes it to my old *Color Me Ugly* partner, Joan Rivers, and she helps him rewrite it. Alexander Cohen is set to produce. I used to go to parties and do a New York Irish guy and it would always break Colodny up. I get a call from Les, who says, "I wrote a play called *Fun City* and I have a confession to make. I used your Irish guy character, but no matter what actor we read, I can't hear it. I only hear you. Would you come to New York and do it?" I tell him, "Les, I'd love to, but I can't come for Actors Equity minimum. I've got a wife and a baby." I get them to pay me $400 a week plus per diem when we're on the road, so it comes to a decent amount.

I fly to New York and I stay in an apartment belonging to Nick Arnold, a brilliantly funny guy with cerebral palsy. One day, he auditions for *The Tonight Show*. They tell him, "Your material is very funny, but we're just not comfortable having you on camera." He tells them, "Okay, so make me a writer," and they do it. Since he's going out to L.A. to work on *The Tonight Show* for a few weeks, he asks if I want stay in his apartment. While he's staying at the Sheraton-Universal, there's an earthquake. I ask him, "Nick, are you okay after the quake?" He says, "I loved it! It was the f-f-first time I walked right!"

In *Fun City*, Gabe Dell plays a concert violinist who is married to Joan Rivers. Rose Marie is Joan's mother and Paul Ford plays a mailman. We rehearse and we go to Washington, D.C. for four weeks at the National Theater. The director, Jerry Adler, has been Alexander Cohen's production manager and this is his first shot at directing. Gabe Dell is a marvelous actor. He's a crazy man and he takes chances like nobody else. In rehearsals, Gabe is over the top all the time. Adler keeps stopping him and sitting on him and I can really see Gabe's frustration. On opening night, he just goes berserk. He climbs the walls. I realize that if an actor functions that way, the smart thing to do is turn him loose and say, "Look, I'll let you go, but at some point, I'll have to pull you back."

Watching Gabe and Adler gives me the understanding of how to work with Robin Williams when I do *Mork & Mindy* years later. I know that if I sit on Robin, it'll be a problem, so I tell him, "Robin, I'm gonna let you go for a couple of days, but at some point, I've gotta stop and pull you back and we gotta do the show."

At one point in the play, Gabe comes home from the symphony all beaten up and his violin's gone. He says, "I got mugged and they broke my Stradivarius." Rose Marie says, "Maybe they heard you play." She never gets a laugh with it. She goes to Jerry Adler and asks, "What's wrong? Why aren't I getting a laugh here? It's not working." She's getting very frustrated, so I tell her, "I'm gonna run out into the audience and listen. Maybe I can find out what's wrong with it." I go out, I watch the scene and I come back and tell her, "It's simple. Just touch his cheek when you say the line. A little affection." The audience feels bad for Gabe when she snaps, "Maybe they heard you play." They think it's nasty. Sure enough, it works. Jerry Adler doesn't work out as a director, but he becomes a very successful actor, eventually playing Hesh Rabkin, the Jewish mob guy on *The Sopranos*.

J.J. Barry and I play the cops that question Gabe. I know J.J. from The Improv in New York. Each night, as we make our entrance, J.J. whispers, "Hey, Howie, do me a favor, will you please? Don't go up tonight," meaning "Don't forget your lines." An actor named Pierre Epstein is playing the doorman. One night, Pierre and I are at the door to the apartment and J.J. is asking Gabe about the guys that beat him up. Suddenly, J.J. drops an entire paragraph that includes an important cue for me to ask Epstein, "Hey, are you the doorman here?" He is supposed to say, "Yes," and I'm supposed to say, "Then go *door*." Pierre and I realize we're in trouble. We're looking at each other thinking, "Oh shit." I walk downstage to J.J. and say, "Why don't you ask him how he met the suspect to begin with?" I'm trying to give him the first line of the paragraph he dropped. J.J. says,

"What?" I say, "Why don't you ask him how he met the suspect to begin with?" J.J. says, "Why don't *you* ask him?" I say, "Okay, I will." So now I'm doing J.J.'s speech and I'm getting laughs. He says, "I'll take over from here," and we get back on track. It's a wonderful moment onstage, because the audience has no idea what's happening. As we're going off, J.J. says to me, "What happened out there? Did you go up?" I tell him, "You fat fuck! Did *I* go up? I saved your ass! You dropped a whole paragraph!" Gabe comes out and as he passes us, he says, "He saved your ass, J.J." He honestly had no idea why I was doing that.

J.J. and I share a suite in the hotel, so I sleep in a bed right next to his. I'm one of those people that when I hit the pillow, I'm out cold. Before I close my eyes each night, I say, "Good night, you guinea bastard." One morning, he says to me, "Y'know, in Italian, there's a saying when someone sleeps like you do. They say it's because he has nothing on his conscience or he's a moron. In your case, you're a moron."

Theatrical legend Abe Burrows comes to see the show. As J.J. and I pass him, Burrows tells us, "You guys are the best thing in the show." In fact, some of the reviews single out J.J. and me. We have two nice scenes, but we get no direction from Jerry Adler. At the end of every rehearsal, we ask, "Any notes?" and he says, "Nah, everything's fine." Finally, we start directing ourselves. If Gabe has a scene with somebody else, I direct it. If I have some stuff, Gabe directs that. The only note I get from the official director is while I'm working on a scene, I can see Edgar Rosenberg whisper into Adler's ear and then Adler tells me, "Howard, don't move when Joan's talking."

We do four weeks in Washington, we come back to New York and do two weeks – and then the show closes. It just doesn't work. It gets terrible reviews. I know from the beginning that despite the title, *Fun City* is a bomb. I'm so sure of it that I take another job in L.A. *before* the play closes. The fact that it's a flop doesn't really bother me, because I am *thrilled* to be on Broadway. That's my big dream – to be in a Broadway show – and there I am, on Broadway!

Flop or no flop, we have a lot of fun.

CHAPTER NINETEEN

After *Fun City* closes, I return to our improv class in L.A. to find that in the short time I'm away, Gary Goodrow has managed to lose most of our students. I tell him, "This is not working. I left you with twenty students. I come back and there are two." I replace Gary with Kathryn Ish. She and I bring the class size back up, but then she leaves, so I'm on my own. I have a great class. Carole King is one of my students. "Tapestry" has come out and she's a musical star, but she wants to be an actress. She recommends Joni Mitchell, but Joni is afraid of improv. I spend an hour on the phone with her, but I can't get her to give my class a shot. Harrison Ford comes for about a month, but he just can't cut it and he drops out.

Comedian Sammy Shore takes my improv workshop. He calls me one day and says, "I need some advice. I've been given a room to use for comedians to perform, but I'm afraid if I open this place, people will think I'm leaving the business." I tell him, "You can still go out and do dates, but you'd be crazy not to do it, because there's no place on the West Coast for people to perform comedy like that." The Improv has yet to open a West Coast branch. I tell Sammy, "Listen, guys like Rodney and Jackie Mason come out here and they need a place to get up and try six or seven minutes that they want to do on Carson. This is the perfect kind of place. With those kind of people coming in, the room is gonna become very popular." He says, "Okay," and he opens The Comedy Store with Rudy de Luca, who writes for Mel Brooks.

I'm onstage opening night of The Comedy Store in 1972. I do a few minutes about mob-owned clubs on the East Coast and then we do a takeoff on the Johnny Mann Singers. There's about fifteen or twenty comics onstage, whistling – and none of us can whistle. There's Pat McCormick, Jack Riley, Tom Poston, Buck Henry – a load of us, whistling "God Bless America," terribly. At one point,

Pat McCormick stands on a bench and it caves in, sending him crashing to the ground. We get loads of laughs.

I wind up teaching the improv class for about four or five years. Long after, I unearth my old waiting list and see the name "David Letterman" written on it. He never got into my class. I wonder whatever became of him...

In addition to teaching improv, I'm trying to get a few projects off the ground. One of them is a TV pilot I write with comedian Stanley Myron Handelman called *Sing For Your Supper*. It's sort of a *Route 66*-type show with two performers, a singer-comic and a piano player, as the lead characters. One's black; the other's white. I take it to Scoey Mitchell, who did such a great job on the demo of *The First Black President*. I figure he might want to be one of the two stars. He tells me he wants to produce it and change the name to *B.C. & Me*, but there is no further discussion of the project. Two months later, I pick up a copy of "Variety" that says, "Comedian Scoey Mitchell has produced a pilot called *B.C. & Me*." He got a group of doctors and lawyers and money people to back it and then he shot the pilot. Even though the pilot is never sold, I sue Scoey and I win. The judgment is for $2,000 of which Scoey pays me $250 and then disappears. Even though I don't get any real money, I'm satisfied. Had the show been a hit, it would've been another story entirely.

One of the guys in my improv class is an attorney named Paul Lichtman. He shows me some stuff he's written and I think he's very good and very funny, so we decide to try writing scripts together to break into television. Ideally, you go in and pitch a couple of ideas to the producers and if there's something they find interesting, they ask you to do a three- or four-page story outline and then they have to pay you. At the time, it's about $1500 for an outline, but it doesn't cost them anything to have that first meeting and listen to your ideas. We make a list of everybody we know in the business. Everybody we know refuses to let us come in and pitch. They figure if we don't have a track record, we aren't worth their time.

I tell Paul, "We've run out of people we know. Why don't we go for broke and go after the biggest guy in the business and let *him* tell us no?" I call Norman Lear, whom I had met but don't really know, and he takes the call. I tell him, "I'm writing with a partner and we have some really good story ideas for *All in the Family* and we'd love to come in and pitch." He says, "Not a problem." Norman sets up a meeting with director/producer John Rich, writer Don Nichols, producer Mickey Ross and his partner Bernie West. We pitch a story where Archie agrees to let Edith throw him a birthday party. He comes home from work and sees a big banner across the living room that says "HAPPY 50th!" and he goes nuts. He thinks it's only his forty-ninth and he denies that it's his fiftieth. He refuses to go to his own birthday party, so he goes to a bar and gets drunk. They buy the story. We call it "Archie's 50th Birthday," but they change the title to "Archie Feels Left Out."

Now that we've written an episode of *All in the Family*, all the people who wouldn't see us before are suddenly calling us: "We'd like you to come in and pitch." We go to *Newhart* and sell them on a story we call "Clink Shrink," which turns out to be the first time Henry Winkler stars in a sitcom episode. In the story, Bob decides he's going to give up watching Monday night football to work with an ex-con and help him adjust to life on the outside. Then he panics and thinks, "What am I doing? What if a *murderer* comes into my office?" He's in the lobby with Peter Bonerz, who plays the dentist, and every time a tough-looking guy gets off the elevator, he walks towards Newhart then he veers off and goes into the dentist's office. Finally, off the elevator comes this little, gentle, sweet guy, Henry Winkler, who happens to be a thief. He asks Newhart, "How can you give up your Mondays? Aren't you a football fan?" Newhart says, "I love football, but I decided I really wanted to do this." Henry asks, "Why don't you tape the games so you can watch them later?" Newhart says, "I don't have a VCR." Henry shows up with a brand-new VCR still in the carton. At the end of the show, he's sitting in the office, waiting to see Newhart. He's handcuffed to a detective, so back to jail he goes.

After *All in the Family* and *Newhart*, we snag a *Partridge Family*. Paul Lichtman has a great eye for story ideas and he comes up with one where Shirley Jones dates a Henry Kissinger-type diplomat. All during their date, he's carrying around a red phone – the hotline – and he's always talking to the White House, so she tells him,

"I just can't do this." He promises that next time, he won't have the phone, but when she makes dinner for him, there's an important diplomatic problem and he misses the call.

Paul is an obsessive writer. I walk back and forth and spit out ideas for jokes and lines and funny bits as they come to me, while Paul sits at the typewriter, hammering away. We rent an office and we go in every day at ten o'clock and work till five, but he goes home and knocks out twelve pages by himself, because he just can't stop. In the morning, he brings them in and I read through them, saying, "This gag's great, but I don't think this one's gonna work." He gets insulted and says, "Why don't *you* write ten pages?" I tell him, "Paul, I don't *want* to write ten pages. I want to come in, write with you, then go home and enjoy my life." He asks, "Would you agree that I write more than you do?" I tell him, "Yes, based on the fact that you do ten, twelve pages at home, you write more than I do." He says, "Then don't you think it'd be fair if we made it sixty/forty? I get sixty and you get forty?" I tell him, "I've got a better idea, Paul. You take *a hundred percent*, 'cause I'm going home." I put my stuff in a box and I leave and that's the end of our collaboration.

To keep money coming in, I continue getting small acting parts. After all, I have a wife and son to provide for. I get a small role in *Steelyard Blues*, which shoots in late 1972. The director is Alan Myerson, my pal from The Committee. He uses almost every one of us in that film. I get a call to come up to Modesto, where they're shooting. No one sends me a script, but I figure since we all do improv, we'll make up the lines on the spot. I have a scene with Peter Boyle and Gary Goodrow, who are playing two crazy guys living in the façade of a house. I'm a health inspector from the city that comes to tell them they can't live there anymore. I knock on the door of the façade and Gary sticks his head around the side and goes back in and then the door opens and Peter and Gary are inside. It's a funny scene, but the information I'm expected to rattle off is very detailed and technical, all about violations of various state and city ordinances. I get to the set and they hand me a script, telling me I'm shooting my scene that day. I tell them, "I thought we were going to improvise." Alan says, "Don't worry about it. We'll shoot something else today and shoot your scene tomorrow." I go back to the hotel, learn the lines, come back the next day and we shoot it.

Jane Fonda and Donald Sutherland are the stars and they are also an item romantically, having just finished *Klute*. After the first couple of days of shooting, they get into a fight, they break up and they aren't talking to each other, so there's a constant feeling of discomfort on the set from that point on.

The Manchu Eagle Murder Caper Mystery, released in 1975, is a takeoff on *The Maltese Falcon* with a great cast that includes my *Fun City* pal Gabe Dell, plus Huntz Hall, Jackie Coogan, Dick Gautier, Vincent Gardenia, Will Geer, Sorrell Booke and Joyce Van Patten. The writer and director is Dean Hargrove, for whom I'd done an episode of *Owen Marshall*. Gabe Dell's character is a mail-order private detective who lives with his wife, played by Joyce. Vincent Gardenia plays a gangster and I play his son, Freddie the Spitter. If somebody says something I don't like, I spit on their shoes. We live on a farm and we raise pigs. There's a scene where I have to go in to feed the pigs. The animal wrangler tells me, "Don't let the pigs knock you down. If they come close and push at you, kick 'em, because if they knock you down, they'll all attack you and eat you." I do a *lot* of kicking that day.

It's great sitting around the set with all those guys, waiting to shoot, hearing their stories. Jackie Coogan is the one that really interests me because of his vaudeville background and working with Chaplin and how his parents beat him for all his money. Huntz Hall tells me about when the Dead End Kids were doing one of my favorite movies, *Angels With Dirty Faces*. They start fooling around one day and Jimmy Cagney slaps Huntz and says, "Hey! Let's be professional here." Cagney comes back the next day and none of the guys will talk to him. Finally, the second or third day, Cagney says, "Alright, alright! I *apologize!*" Things are okay after that.

I could support myself as a standup, but I prefer acting and my goal is to be a regular on a TV series. In the summer of 1975, I get as close as I'll ever come to achieving that goal. *Flannery and Quilt* is a wonderful pilot for NBC directed by the brilliant Carl Reiner, written by Carl and Marty Feldman. Red Buttons is an Irish street guy – an ex-prize fighter who tends bar. My friend, actress and singer Pat Finley, is cast as Red's daughter. She recommends me to play her fiancé, Kevin Caselli.

When I go in to read for Carl, I ask if I can talk a little about the character. He says, "Sure." I tell him, "Y'know, I come from that same background. I know a lot of Italian guys from Little Italy. Most of them have nicknames the family always calls them. I think it might be nice if, rather than Kevin, his name is Sonny." Carl agrees and writes a lovely joke. Pat introduces me to Red and says, "Pop, this is my fiancé, Kevin." I tell him, "All my friends and family call me Sonny. You can call me Sonny, if you like." Red says, "Thanks, Kevin." It's a simple little joke that works. Carl is so good at that.

I get a thousand dollars for my role in the pilot, which is terrific. In my head, I can't help but "extrapolate" that into $22,000 – assuming the show is picked up for a full season. I think about finally getting a better car. Anita is thrilled at the possibility of good, steady money coming into the family. I tell Carl, "If the series goes on the air, I'd like to direct some of them." He's open to that. NBC only has one open slot in their schedule, but instead of giving it to *Flannery and Quilt*, they pick up *The Montefuscos*, a short-lived sitcom written by my friends Sam Denoff and Bill Persky. My dreams of being a regular on a series evaporate and my debut as a TV director is delayed – but not for long.

CHAPTER TWENTY

In the early seventies, Paul Kent, my old friend from the Desilu Players, asks me if I would direct a play at his theater – the Melrose Theater in West Hollywood – even though I've never directed before. It's a two-character play starring Jim Connell and Joan Darling with a long, ridiculous title, something like *Don't Walk on the Grass on Sunday Unless Your Mother's Leaving on Tuesday*. There's a moment in the play where Jim says, "I'm normal" and Joan says, "Normal doesn't mean perfect." We tell the writer, "*That's* the title! It's right there in your own play." He tells us, "No, I'm not gonna change it."

Paul is Brooklyn Italian. He says, "Let's fake a New York hit. We take him and threaten him." I'm game. We get in the car, Paul's driving, and the writer – a very WASPy guy – is sitting next to Paul. I'm in the back. It's about seven-thirty at night and it's getting dark. We pull into an alley and Paul says, "Have you thought about the title?" He says, "Yeah, I'm not gonna change it." Paul tells him, "You don't change it, I'm gonna kill ya." The guy starts to laugh, so I say, "Why are you laughing? He's serious. If you don't change the title, we're gonna kill you and put you in the trunk of the car, drive out to the desert and bury you. They'll never hear from you again." He panics and says, "Okay! Okay! I'll change the title!" He does change it – but we had to go through all that just to get him to do it.

Normal Doesn't Mean Perfect goes very smoothly, so Paul asks me to direct *Room Service*, the classic Allen Boretz/John Murray comedy that was made into a popular Marx Brothers movie in 1938. That goes well, too. In 1974, Paul tells me he's going on the road in a show called *Father's Day* and asks me if I would take over his theater for him. I happily accept the challenge. The next play on the theater's agenda is Neil Simon's *Star-Spangled Girl*, a three-character comedy about a girl who comes to San Francisco from the Midwest. I start rehearsing it and about fours days in, I realize it isn't a very good play. I don't think it's funny and I can't figure out a way to make it work, but it's Neil Simon! Where do I get off saying Neil Simon's play isn't any good? I'm going nuts worrying about how to make it work and I'm willing to try anything. What if I have the guy play the girl's part and the girl play the guy's part? At one point, I consider having them do it in blackface!

One night, I wake up about two in the morning and I can't fall back asleep. I turn on the TV and there's Edwin Newman interviewing – of all people – Neil Simon! Newman asks him, "Do you sit down and say, 'I gotta think about an idea for a play' or does the idea just come to you and then you write it?" Simon says, "The idea always comes to me first and then I write it. The only time that didn't happen was *Star-Spangled Girl*. I felt I *needed* to write a play, so I sat there trying to figure it out. My plays are always about New York, but with that one, I was in an area that didn't have the same feel to it: San Francisco and a woman from the Midwest. Of all my plays, I think that one is the least important."

Next day, I get to the theater and I tell the three actors, "I just heard from Neil Simon. He thinks the play's a dud and so do I. We're gonna find something else, but I promise you, the three of you will be in it. If there's a play you've always wanted to do, bring it in." One of the actors, Alan McCrea, says, "There's a play I love called *Where Has Tommy Flowers Gone?* by Terrence McNally." I'm already a big fan of McNally, so I tell him, "Great. Let me read it." I do and I think it's terrific. Then they tell me Paul Kent *hates* the play and he already turned it down when somebody else wanted to do it. I tell them, "He's just gonna have to live with it, because that's the play we're doing."

No sooner do I make the decision to do the play than I realize I have a big problem. The play has *twelve sets*. It has a Howard Johnson's, a scene in front of Bloomingdale's, a scene in a cab, a supermarket, an apartment, a den in someone's house in Florida, an airplane. It's very complicated. In the New York production, they use rear projection to suggest the various locations, but we can't afford that. I confer with my set designer, Newell Alexander, to see how we can solve this challenge.

I take one of my improv students, Bill Kirchenbauer – a very talented guy who later gets his own sitcoms, *Growing Pains* and *Just the Ten Of Us* – and I ask him if he could be like a Chinese property man, working in all black and coming onstage in pantomime to set each scene for the audience. He's cool with that. I tell Bill, "We'll have an empty stage with just a few chairs." For one scene, I need to have three bathroom stalls in a Bloomingdale's bathroom. We have a skyline design on the wall in the front and on both sides, but the upstage wall is on wheels, so we wheel it around and there are sinks and mirrors painted on it. The three stalls are already there.

For the supermarket, I have Bill enter the store with an imaginary cart, going down the aisle, picking out imaginary items and putting them into his cart. Downstage is the produce section where he pretends to have trouble opening up a plastic produce bag. Then the principals enter. I have Bill do the same sort of pantomime on the plane, opening up the overhead compartment and putting his suitcase up top and sitting in the seat. We have simple, straight-back cane chairs, but he acts like he's reclining in an airline seat. Bill sets the different scenes all throughout the play, which really enhances the production. In fact, it turns out much better than if we used rear projection.

One actor doubles as our lighting director. I tell him, "There's a part in the play for you, but it's a dog. Are you interested?" He says, "Sure." I have a friend named Michael Mann – a manager, not the director – who has a big, hairy dog, like a German shepherd. I call Michael and I tell him, "I have an actor who's going to be playing a dog and I want him to spend a lot of time with yours. He'll walk the dog, go to the park, whatever." I tell the actor, "Don't come near the theater for two weeks. Go hang out with Michael's dog and *become* that dog." He goes off for two weeks to study dog. We take a sweatshirt and sweatpants and dye them brown. We cut up a T-shirt and make it into a tail and a roll of fur for around his neck. He gets great reviews. Everybody is knocked out by his dog performance. The problem is, he's upstaging everybody, being adorable and scratching and doing all those dog things. But *Where Has Tommy Flowers Gone?* gets *great* reviews.

Valerie Harper's ex-husband, Dick Schaal, is a wonderful impro-viser. She would come to see The Committee at the Tiffany Theater, so I get to know Valerie. One day, I tell her, "Y'know, that charac-ter you're doing on *The Mary Tyler Moore Show* – Rhoda – is not Jewish. She's Italian." She says, "You're right! I'm doing my step-mother who's an Italian from Jersey. How did you know?" I tell her, "There's a different sound from an Italian woman that speaks English fluently and a Jewish woman that speaks English fluently. Everybody refers to 'a New York accent,' but there are loads of New York accents." I do my Irish guy and then my Italian guy and then my Jewish guy. She appreciates the differences.

When MTM spins *Rhoda* off into a separate series in 1974, I tell Valerie I want to direct, so she and Dave Davis, one of the show's producers, bring me in to be part of a program for prospective directors. I already know Dave, because his daughter, Abby, goes to school with my son, Anthony, and they play together. Through-out the first season of *Rhoda*, I'm one of five potential directors who go to MTM, sit in the bleachers with our mouths shut, and observe every day of rehearsals. We aren't allowed to go on the stage or bother the director with questions. Among the other guys are Tony Mordente and Asaad Kelada, who become very successful directors. The guy directing *Rhoda* is a wonderful actor and director named Robert Moore. He and I once did a commercial together in New York for Colgate Lime Shaving Cream. Bob Moore is set to do every episode of *Rhoda* for however long the series lasts, so none of us feels like we really have a shot at directing any of them.

During hiatus, when I'm doing *Where Has Tommy Flowers Gone?*, I invite everybody at *Rhoda* to come by and see the play – producers Allan Burns and Jim Brooks, and Valerie. They all come. The next day, Allan calls me and says, "I thought the play was wonderful and I thought your work was great. Can I read the script? I want to see what you did with it." He reads the play and he sees that I took out all the rear projection and added the pantomime character to set each scene. He's impressed with all that I'd brought to the play, but it doesn't mean a whole lot, because Bob Moore is directing every *Rhoda*.

Then one day, Bob Moore is asked to direct the Neil Simon movie *Murder By Death,* so he wants out of his *Rhoda* contract. Suddenly, they need someone to start the new season. I'm in bed and I get a phone call from Allan Burns. He says, "We'd like you to do the first two episodes." I tell him, "That's *great*! Thank you, Allan!" I hang up and then it hits me: "I can't do this. I'm full of crap. What do I know about directing? I've been telling everyone how much I want to direct, but I don't know cameras from my ass." The weekend before I'm to direct my first episode, my former improv student, Carole King, invites me to a James Taylor concert at the Greek Theatre telling me, "I'm going to be a surprise guest star and I'd love for you to come and see it." I say, "Are you kidding? I'd love to!" She gives me four tickets, so I take Anita and the two boys. I'm sitting there watching this terrific show and all of a sudden, I get palpitations. I break out in a cold sweat and I'm panicked about going in on Monday. They're going to find out I'm a fake. The directing career I've wanted for years is over before it begins.

I'm sitting at the Greek Theatre thinking, "I'll feign a heart attack and tell them I'm in the hospital and I can't do the show. But once I blow this, I've got to figure out what I'm going to do for a living." I start going over what jobs I could do and I don't know why, but the only job that keeps popping into my head is shoe salesman! That's the menu: Either I become a television director or I become a shoe salesman. So I think, "There's no way I'm gonna be a *shoe salesman,* so I guess I'm gonna go and do this!"

I make the decision to follow through on directing *Rhoda* – but I still don't know cameras from my ass. There's a wonderful cinematographer on *Rhoda* named Kenny Peach, an old-timer who's done tons of movies. He likes me and he's *extremely* helpful. He's like Til Gabani on *Take the Money and Run.* I always find some way to charm those guys, because they've done this a hundred times. My position as director might *sound* important, but they already know every trick in the book.

There's a grip that works with Kenny, another old-timer, who asks me, "You're gonna be directing, right? I don't do this often, but I like you, so I'm gonna give you some advice. They're gonna ask you a lot of questions. Don't *ever* tell them you don't know, because you'll scare the hell out of them. If they ask you, 'Do you want the blue jacket or the red jacket?' don't hesitate. Pick a jacket. It makes no difference which color. You don't like it later on, you change the color, 'cause you're the director and you can do that. But you can't say, 'I don't know' or you'll scare the hell out of them." I tell Valerie this and we start breaking up about picking the red jacket or the blue jacket. First day on the set, the camera coordinator asks me, "Where do you want Camera B?" I blurt out, "*Red jacket!*" and Valerie screams.

Those old guys are very helpful. Kenny Peach takes pictures of the stand-ins with a 100mm camera at twelve feet away, then at fourteen feet, then a two-shot at twenty-two feet. He gives me all these pictures and on the back, he marks the lens and the distance. It's like those notebooks I kept on *Take the Money and Run* and *Bananas* with all the camera shots and lenses and so forth, except now it's multi-cameras instead of just one. I study it all and that's really how I learn to direct. There's a woman named Mai-Britt Santacroce who's been Ingmar Bergman's editor for years. She marries actor Gerald Mohr and she doesn't want to travel back and forth to Sweden, so she takes a job as script supervisor on American TV shows, including *Rhoda*. She teaches me so much. On the first show, I need to do a quick pickup shot of one line, so I say, "Okay, get the camera ready and just say that one line. That's all we need." She whispers in my ear, "Have him come through the door and finish the shot when he sits down and *then* cut." I tell her, "But I don't need all that stuff before and after. I just need him to say the line." Mai says, "Just do it now and we'll have lunch tomorrow and I'll explain." We have lunch and she explains why you have to shoot a little extra before and after to give you the leeway to cut it right. I ask her questions all the time and she's very open, very helpful. I learn a *lot* about editing from her.

The *Rhoda* cast has already been doing the show for a season, so they know their characters well. You can't start telling them about their characters, but you can help them with a joke. David Groh, who plays Valerie's husband, is a good actor, but not a particularly funny performer. I think they should never have made Rhoda someone's wife, because once she's married, she's off the market.

If she's still dating, you have all those wonderful story possibilities, but marriage locks her in. In one scene, David Groh has a line and it doesn't get a laugh. Jim Brooks, Allan Burns and I are trying to figure it out. David and Valerie are in the living room and David is seated when he says the line. I tell Jim, "Why don't we have him stand up and say it?" David stands up and says the line and Jim says, "That's it!" The line works. We don't know why; it just does.

A few years later, I'm doing a show called *Best of the West*. Tom Ewell, a real pro, plays a drunken doctor in a saloon. It's a typical Western setup with a bar downstairs and rooms upstairs with saloon girls. The guest star is walking up the steps. He turns and says something and it gets a laugh. I tell him, "Do me a favor. Instead of turning the normal way, turn *this* way and say your line," and I demonstrate how he should make a complete turn in the other direction. He does the turn and it gets a much bigger laugh. He asks me, "Why is that funnier?" I tell him, "I don't know." He says, "What do you mean you don't know? You told me to do it!" I tell him, "It's instinct. I can't explain why it's funnier." I go to Tom Ewell, who co-starred in *The Seven Year Itch*, and I ask him, "Why is that funnier?" He tells me, "I've been doing comedy for fifty years and I have no idea why anything is funny."

Despite my fear of directing, the first episode goes smoothly. Of course, I'm working with the likes of Valerie Harper, Nancy Walker, Harold Gould and Julie Kavner. When you have a great cast like that, you don't have to do much. They know what they're doing and the writers are great. My main concern is handling the cameras and doing the right things with them – knowing where the camera is to make sure the joke is covered. For example, if there is a joke about someone's eyeglasses, I know I shouldn't be in a wide shot of the whole room. We wrap the first episode, I'm in line for food at the commissary and Allan Burns tells me, "My partner agrees with me and we'd like you to do four more." I say, "That's great," and I wind up directing a total of six episodes of *Rhoda* for MTM, which is a terrific place to work.

Once I start directing, I find that I like it better than acting. There's a certain control – and I'm something of a control freak. You're in charge and there's a kind of respect and an aura about being the director. Even as I enjoy the control and the respect, I make fun of it. I insist that the cast call me "Mr. Director Sir Honey." Someone gifts me with a pair of socks that have "Mr. Director" stitched onto the left one and "Sir Honey" on the right one. In terms of my approach to directing, my feeling about a master shot is that it gives you geography. It gives you a sense of the set, where everything is. I don't like to stay off a master too long. Every second page, I'll look to go back to a master so the audience can see where everything is. When you're in tight shots, you can't tell where people and things are in relation to each other, so I like to use the master for geography.

While I'm finishing up the fifth *Rhoda*, Allan recommends me for the Barnard Hughes sitcom *Doc*, because they're having trouble finding a director they're happy with. I watch them tape a show and then, when I come in for the read-through on my episode, I tell the actors, "The show is wonderful, but in my mind, it doesn't end until after curtain calls and what I saw was very sloppy bows." Barnard says, "Oh my God, someone who cares about theater!" I tell him, "That's the first thing I want to rehearse." Everybody is in awe of Barney. He's such a good actor and such a pro, you can't help but be impressed with him. Elizabeth Wilson, his wonderful co-star, is the same way. They're theater people. They're doing this because it's big money, probably the most they'll ever make. You don't get that kind of money onstage, but it allows Barney to go back to New York after the show and do *Da*.

Doc also stars the venerable Mary Wickes, who plays the nurse and who drives me absolutely *crazy*. She enters Barnard's office, then stops and turns and asks me, "Why am I coming in here?" I think fast and tell her, "You're going in to sharpen a pencil for him." She constantly questions why she is entering a room. It's not the director's job to do that: You're an actor. *You* figure out why you're going in. She just drives me crazy. Eventually, I have the prop guy give me a pencil, a letter, a half-eaten sandwich, whatever. As soon as she asks why she's going into a room, I walk over and put the plate down and tell her, "It's lunchtime, so you're bringing a sandwich to him" or "The pencil's broken and you need to sharpen it." I have five or six things she can do, so as soon as she asks me why she's going somewhere, I walk up and say, "Here! You're gonna give him the pen!" One day, we're shooting in front of a live audience. Mary stops and turns and asks, "Why am I going in here?" Barnard says, "Because if you don't come in, I'll be talking to myself."

On my first episode, the cast is running the scene. I'm watching and the scene is fine. I start thinking to myself, "They're gonna think I'm not directing," so I make up a bullshit piece of direction and I give it to them. I get into my car that night and I'm driving home and I feel so guilty. I think, "Why did I do that? I'm never going to do that again." If the scene is going right, it doesn't need direction. Leave them alone. That incident turns out to be a great help to me as I continue my new career as a director.

In another episode, Steve Martin guest stars as Barnard Hughes' son. The role is supposed to be played by Billy Crystal, but he's off in New York doing Howard Cosell's variety show, so he can't do it. Personally, I don't think Billy's right for it and Steve Martin looks more like he'd be Barnard Hughes' son, with his light hair and fair skin. Steve Martin is a priest who wants to be a standup comic, so they all go to see him at a comedy club in the Village, with a wall of bricks behind the stage. I tell Steve, "When I was working the hungry i with the brick wall behind me, I would always say to the audience, 'You're probably wondering why there's a brick wall. That's so if you get bored with my act, you can count the bricks.'" Steve uses that line in the show. I hire Improv-owner Budd Friedman for what turns out to be his first TV show. He plays the emcee of the comedy club. Big stretch, right?

On another episode, Doc is going out of business and he has to sell his clinic. I hire my pal Gabe Dell as a guy who's going to turn the clinic into a delicatessen. The model Gabe uses for his character is Max Asnas, owner of the Stage Deli, who is a great character in his own right. Max sees himself as a Yiddish actor on Second Avenue, but he isn't. He wears a camelhair wraparound coat, fedora with the wide brim, the whole look. Gabe's character comes into the clinic and says, "I've gotta measure how long the distance is here," and he puts his arms straight out to measure the distance from the wall across the room. "Okay, six feet, twelve feet," and he's twirling front to back to front to back with every measurement, holding his arms straight out. Then he stops and says, "Corned beef here, potato salad there." Just like with *Fun City*, Gabe is constantly over the top in rehearsal, so the producers come to me and say, "I don't know about this guy. Maybe we should replace him." I tell them, "That's his way of working. He'll be fine. I'll bring him down." It works out fine and Gabe is hilarious on that show, spinning and twirling around the room.

Steve Guttenberg is also in that episode – as an extra. We're doing a scene and there's something about him that tells me he's more than just an extra, so I say, "Listen, do you want me to find some business for you to do in this scene?" That means he'd get another thirty bucks or so. He says, "No, my agents don't know I'm doing this. I'm an actor, but I'm broke, so I'm doing extra work. My agents told me they don't want me doing this, so I don't want to be seen." I tell him, "Okay, here's what you do: It's a clinic. People are sitting on benches. Sit in the last row. It's winter. Pull the scarf across your face, pull your hat down and just sit there and no one will know who it is." Years later, I'm directing *Pecos Bill: King of the Cowboys* for *Tall Tales & Legends* and I hire Steve Guttenberg for the title role. We're on the set the first day and Steve says, "I worked with you before." I ask him, "Where? I don't remember that." He says, "I was an extra on an episode of *Doc* and you were very nice to me." I find that show and look at it and sure enough, there's Steve Guttenberg sitting in the back row with a scarf across his face and a woolen hat pulled down over his head.

I wind up directing seven episodes of *Doc* with the promise of directing the rest of the season – twenty-two shows – but ABC decides they're going to switch from shooting the show on film to videotaping it, because it's cheaper. I have no experience directing a taped show, which is a vastly different process – sitting in the control booth and calling cameras – than directing a filmed show down on the set, like a movie. I tell them I want to continue directing *Doc*, but I need to learn how to direct for videotape. They agree to let me direct a ninth show with an option for the remainder of the season, in the event the series is picked up.

I spend a lot of time in control booths watching experienced video directors. The Technical Director turns to me and asks, "Are you

the new Assistant Director?" I say, "No, I don't know enough to be
an Assistant Director. I'm a director." Everybody laughs and that
endears me to them, which I need, because you depend on those
guys when you don't really know what you're doing. I sit in that
booth and I watch and learn. I sit behind Tony Mordente at MTM,
I sit behind Hal Cooper at Norman Lear's company, I sit behind
Jack Shea and Peter Baldwin. Those guys are terrific. They really
snap those shots off from one camera to the next like it's nothing.
They're very open and very helpful and I learn a lot from them.

I'm very lucky to have experienced crew people around me that
are willing to help and they're so kind to me – except for one guy.
After wrapping the first *Doc*, I'm asked to do a videotaped pilot
starring John Byner for ABC and I'm not really ready. I need more
experience working in a control booth on a taped show. With film,
you depend on Assistant Directors and camera operators and those
guys are good. On *Rhoda*, they're great. But on this John Byner
pilot, the Technical Director in the booth is an older guy and he
will not push a button unless I call the shot and snap my fingers. I
tell him, "Listen, if I don't get the shot, just push the button." He
won't do it. He's impossible. I go to Tiffany and I buy him a really
nice pen, hoping he'll be nicer and more willing to be helpful. It
does nothing. He leaves me hanging and the pilot is a disaster.

From there on, the guys are helpful. I tell them, "Listen, I'm new
at this, so if I don't call a shot and you know it's coming up, please
call it." After I get a little more comfortable literally calling the
shots, I tell them, "If I put my hand out, don't call the shot until
I snap my fingers." If there's a laugh, I hold my hand up and wait
for the laugh to subside and then I snap my fingers to take another
angle, because as helpful as the Technical Directors are, I know
comedy timing. It's just like when my father held my sleeve before
I said the next line. I direct the ninth episode of *Doc* – my first
one on tape – which turns out to be the final episode of the series.
Minimum for directing at that time is $3500 per show and so I
make $32,000 that year, which is the most money I ever made and
I'm absolutely thrilled.

Next up is a popular spinoff of *Happy Days*, a series my former
writing partner Paul Lichtman and I once wrote a story for.

CHAPTER TWENTY-ONE

On *Rhoda* and *Doc*, my boss is Grant Tinker, who never gets involved creatively; only from a business standpoint. People ask him creative questions and he answers, "I have no idea. Talk to the writers. They'll know." He says his talent is recognizing talent: Hire the right people and then leave them alone. Everybody loves Grant. He's the best guy to work for. After *Rhoda* and *Doc*, people know there's a new director in town. I'm the hot guy – for a little while. All my agent does is take calls. One is from Garry Marshall's office, saying he wants me to direct three episodes of *Laverne & Shirley*, which is in its first season.

Like Grant Tinker, Garry Marshall is a great guy to work with. He's an amazing man with a great sense of what works and what the public wants to see. At one point, he has *five* shows on the air at the same time! Garry's very easy. He's only hands-on if you have a problem. Nevertheless, directing *Laverne & Shirley* turns out to be a difficult experience, mostly because of dealing with Penny Marshall and, to a lesser degree, Cindy Williams. I already know Cindy from when she was a secretary to producer Fred Roos. She would often come around to watch The Committee, because she wanted to be in show business.

On one show, there's a scene that takes place in their apartment after dark. The door opens and Cindy is walking backwards and there's a guy with his arms around her, kissing her. They land on the couch and boom – you hear Laverne. She's underneath the guy. She sits up and says, "Oh, hi, Shirley, this is my friend Frank," and she introduces him. I tell Penny, "Stay down. Don't get up. Introduce them from a prone position. It's funnier that way." Penny says, "Yeah, but that's not real." I say, "What do you mean it's not real? It's funny. We're doing comedy. You lying there the whole time and saying, "Shirley, this is my friend, Frank. Frank, this is Shirley," instead of getting up and saying it is funnier." Penny argues with me. Lenny and Squiggy – Michael McKean and David Lander – are standing off to the side and they're whispering to Penny, "Howard's right." She agrees to do it the way I suggest, but that kind of thing happens a lot on the show, mostly with Penny.

There's another scene where Penny is crying and blowing her nose. She puts the tissue back in her purse after she blows her nose. I tell her, "Y'know, that's really disgusting. Put the tissue on the table or in an ashtray or something, but don't put it back in your purse." She says, "But it's funny." I tell her, "It's not funny, it's tasteless." We go back and forth over that and she says, "I'll bet you it'll get a laugh." I tell her, "You know what? I can drop my pants and it'll get a laugh, but it's still tasteless."

Another ongoing problem is Cindy's concern that because Penny is Garry's sister, she gets more lines, more jokes, more to do on the show. Cindy's manager is a very nice lady named Patricia McQueeney. Cindy has Patricia sitting in the audience, counting the words! Then you have a situation where one of the stars won't come out of her dressing room until the other one comes out. I say, "Cindy, we need you on the set," and she says, "Is Penny out there?" I tell her, "No." She says, "Well, I'm not coming out until *she* comes out." It's childish.

Nevertheless, Penny and Cindy have great chemistry. They're both funny. They can both do physical comedy. They're terrific and it's a shame that they have this petty craziness going on. We do some wonderful stuff on that series. On one show, Laverne and Shirley are candy stripers that volunteer at a hospital. They have to change the bedding on a big, heavyset guy that's out cold. We put together a physical thing that I think is as good as anything you'd see on *I Love Lucy*. Before Cindy enters, I tell Penny, "You know how a magician pulls the tablecloth off a table and everything stays? You say to the guy, 'Nothing up my sleeves' and then grab the sheet and pull and then slide under the bed." She does it and it's a scream. Then she gets into bed behind the guy and uses his back to push against him to make him sit up. As this happens, she slips under and he winds up on top of her. In walks Cindy, who says, "Oh, excuse me," and starts to leave. Shirley yells, "Help!" and Cindy comes back in. Cindy straddles the guy. She's wearing rubber gloves that start to stretch and stretch and stretch, while Penny's hanging on to the finger. They finally get the sheet out from under him and they brush off their hands like they've done a good job and they walk out. It's a great piece of physical comedy that the three of us put together. I think it's every bit as good as Lucy with the candy on the assembly line.

The casting on that show is terrific. Michael McKean and David Lander are a great combination. Two goofy guys. Both of them are very good actors. Later, I do a *Head of the Class* with David playing the principal of the school and he's very funny. Michael turns out to be a very solid actor, Phil Foster is terrific as Laverne's father, and my old friend, the great Betty Garrett, is just a delight to work with.

One week, Penny comes to Garry and complains that she didn't get her check. Garry says, "What do you mean? Paramount sends it out every week." Garry and Penny's dad, Tony Marshall, is the Executive Producer. Garry tells Penny, "Let me check with Pop and see what's going on." He tells Tony, "Dad, Penny didn't get her check this week." Tony says, "I know. She's not getting it, because she was fresh to me. When she apologizes, she'll get her check." Garry says, "Pop, it's not her *allowance*! She's an actress and that's her money! You can't hold back her paycheck! It's $40,000!" Tony says, "She doesn't get it until she apologizes." Garry tells Penny, "He won't give it to you unless you apologize." Penny goes to Tony and says, "I'm sorry, Pop. I didn't mean it." He gives her the check.

I do six episodes of *Laverne & Shirley* and then I take a break to work on a few other shows.

In-between my stints on *Laverne & Shirley*, I direct an episode of *The Cop and the Kid* at Paramount for producer Jerry Davis, who's a great guy. It's about a cop who adopts a black kid off the street and then he has to deal with the kid and all his problems. The series goes away real fast, which is a shame, because it stars Charlie Durning, who's a real pro. Charlie's mother is played by Patsy Kelly, one of the great old-time actresses that did movies with Hal Roach and Thelma Todd.

Then I do three episodes of *Fernwood 2 Night*, a spinoff of *Mary Hartman, Mary Hartman* for Norman Lear. It's a lot of fun and a great takeoff on talk shows. In a way, it's an early version of what would become *The Larry Sanders Show*. The combination of Martin Mull and Fred Willard is terrific. They're perfect for each other, Marty being who he is and Fred playing the dumbest guy you've ever met, always doing or saying something stupid. In one episode, they have a high-school swimming team as guests on their show, but since they don't have a pool, they put the girls on tables and have them pretend they're synchronized swimmers. *Fernwood 2 Night* is a good show and it's a shame they don't keep it running longer. I'm not sure if they aren't getting the audience they want or what, but it's a very special show.

Around this time, I direct a few episodes of the musical sitcom *Sugar Time!*, which is produced by James Komack. It's based on a British show about three girl singers who live together. All three of the actresses are good: Didi Carr, who's sort of a Barbra Streisand-like nightclub singer; Marianne Black, who's a Broadway singer; and Barbi Benton, a former Playmate of the Year. James Komack calls himself "The Chairman of the Board." He's the only person I know who ever calls himself that; everyone else is the *president* of their company, even Norman Lear.

We do one episode where the comedy lead is John David Carson, who co-starred with George C. Scott and Trish Van Devere in a heavy drama. In the show, he's dating one of the girls and he goes to pick her up. She's not ready, so the other two girls are downstairs talking with him and he hits on both of them. Carson is a lovely man, but he's not a comic actor. We do the run-through for Jimmy Komack and it doesn't work. Jimmy tells Carson, "I'm not familiar with your work, but I assume you have a SAG card," which I find really mean-spirited. He starts to tell Carson how Terry Kiser would play it. Terry is a very good comic actor and I just know Jimmy is planning on bringing him in.

After the run-through, Jimmy walks up to me and says, "Fire Carson." I tell him, "I didn't hire him. You did. You fire him. The only call I'm going to make is to call him and say, 'I'm sorry it didn't work out.'" Jimmy fires Carson. Next day, Terry Kiser is there. Jimmy tells Terry, "When you walk into that apartment and the two girls are there, I want you to have the image in mind that you're walking in with your cock in your hand!" I say, "Jimmy, where's he gonna go from there? What's written is subtle and it works, but if he comes on that strong, he has no place to go and the audience is gonna hate him." As usual, Jimmy says, "Do it the way I tell you."

We do two shows, the first in the afternoon, which is the dress rehearsal. Sometimes we use some of the pieces from that in the final show. In the afternoon, there are a lot of old ladies with blue hair in the audience. Terry comes on strong and they hate him. The show is just dreadful. I go into the green room and Jimmy's there, alone and coked-up. He's sitting with a glass of vodka and knocking his ring against the glass with his shaky hand: Ding ding ding ding. The first words out of his mouth are, "You wanna see me get angry?" I tell him, "I don't give a fuck whether you get angry or not. It doesn't affect me." He says, "Oh yeah? You never saw me angry." I ask him, "Jimmy, are you threatening me?" He says, "*You* figure it out!" I tell him, "Jimmy, let me explain something to you: You're a Jew from West End Avenue. Your idea of a fight is to call your lawyer. I'm a Jew from the Lower East Side. I get into a fight with you and I get anywhere near you, I'll bite your nose off. And when I knock you down, I'll kick you until you stop moving." He says, "What are you, crazy?" I tell him, "Yes. Please keep it in mind the next time you threaten me. Now, do you want to talk about the show and stop the macho bullshit?" He says, "Tell me how to fix it." I say, "It's simple. Let him do the scene as written and not come on so strong." Jimmy says, "Okay, fine." I tell Terry, "Don't come on like Jimmy said. Just play the moments, because otherwise, you have no place to go." We do the evening show and it goes great. I walk up to Jimmy and I tell him, "Well, we got a nice show after all." He says, "You and I are on a collision course." I walk away. After shooting another episode, I injure my back and while I'm recuperating at home, I get a phone call telling me I'm fired. It's a crazy business.

I direct an episode of *Busting Loose* for Lowell Ganz. Adam Arkin is the star. It's a smooth experience, but then I direct an episode of *Fish*, a spinoff of *Barney Miller*, which is anything but a smooth experience. The producer, Danny Arnold, is so hands-on, you don't even need to be there. He's one of those guys that likes to redo everything you do. On Friday, he gets a tape of what I shoot, then I sit with him on Sunday and he says, "I think this shot should be a single." I say, "Okay, fine." I shoot the show and then he comes down and reshoots the whole show. His wife and kids are sitting in the bleachers, stopping by on their way to Vegas. At two in the morning, they're still sitting there. He reshoots everything. Everybody knows that Danny Arnold is impossible. No matter who it is he's working with, he has to redo the whole show.

I come back to direct two more episodes of *Laverne & Shirley*. On one of them, "The Quiz Show," I have a run-in with Abe the camera operator. Penny and Cindy are facing each other and there's a table behind each of them with clothes on it. The whole idea is for them to dress each other. I want to see them reaching for the clothes, so I have the camera cutting them around the hips so you can see the table, and then I have a master shot. Abe says it's too wide. I tell him, "It's not too wide. I want the audience to see the table." The night we're shooting it, I'm looking at his camera and I see the lens-puller going in for a closeup, so I yell, "Cut! Abe, I told you the shot I want and I don't want it changed. If you're concerned about them complaining about you, I'll sign a letter saying I *insisted* on it – but don't touch the goddamn lens! I want the shot I set up." After those two episodes, I leave *Laverne & Shirley*. Phil Foster comes on the set after I'm gone and announces, "You know why Howard Storm isn't directing? Because he *directs*!" I was actually *directing*, instead of just giving the stars free rein. I argue with them about what's funny. That's the "mistake" I made, so they don't ask me back.

I leave *Laverne & Shirley*, but I remain on good terms with Garry Marshall, who gives me a shot at a new series he's developing that's yet another spinoff of the ultra-successful *Happy Days*. The show is called *Mork & Mindy* and the gig lasts three years.

CHAPTER TWENTY-TWO

In addition to having worked with Garry Marshall, a point in favor of my getting *Mork & Mindy* is that its young star, Robin Williams, is represented by my old friends, Jack Rollins and Charlie Joffe, who feel that I have "a sense of Robin." I do standup. I'm an actor. I improvise. I have a good understanding of all the things that Robin Williams likes to do. I direct the two-part pilot. Based on that, they offer me the entire season. That turns into three years, which is *unbelievable* in the fickle world of network TV.

We get several shows in the can before they begin to air. Robin and I eat at the Paramount commissary, at Nickodell's next to the studio, and at a Hungarian place around the corner from Paramount. It doesn't matter. Wherever we go, nobody recognizes Robin. Yet. Once *Mork & Mindy* starts to air, everything changes. We have charity softball games to raise money for MDA and every show has its own team. Robin is driving an old, beat-up, two-passenger Triumph. We get to the ball field and Henry Winkler is pitching. The game ends and a few kids run up to Henry to get his autograph. He signs a few and then he takes off.

Then Robin gets out of his beat-up Triumph and goes walking out towards right field. Immediately, the stands empty. Everybody goes rushing out to right field, so our team runs over to protect him. Fans clamor for Robin's autograph and grab at him. The show is coming in first or second in the Nielsens every week and every college in the country, every fraternity and sorority, has Thursday *Mork & Mindy* nights. That charity softball game is our first experience with Robinmania. I tell the fans, "Please go back to the stands!" They don't want to go back. I tell them, "Then stand along the baseline, but don't step over it, because they're trying to play."

We finish the game and once again, everybody comes running at Robin. Our team makes a wedge around him and gets him to his car so he can make his getaway. It's the first time we realize the power of that show and the power of Robin; how big he'd become in a short period of time.

Mork & Mindy becomes the hottest show in the city. Big-time producers call and ask for tickets to the show, because they want to bring their kids. It's amazing. Every Friday night when we shoot the show, it's jam-packed. One day, I get a call from the front office saying, "Ginger Rogers called. She's a big fan of the show and she asked if she could come and watch the rehearsal." I see her sitting in the bleachers, so I walk up and say, "Miss Rogers, I'm Howard Storm. I'm the director." She says, "I know who you are! I watch the show every week! You're wonderful!" Legendary Western director Henry Hathaway also asks to come to the show. They're just in awe of Robin.

The character of Mork is sweet and totally naïve, like a child. He takes everything literally. You tell him, "Zip it up!" and he looks down at his pants. You tell him, "Go jump in a lake!" and he looks for a lake to jump into. Robin's brilliance in becoming this character is that he can do almost anything. He can play hurt and the audience wants to cry. He has that effect. He's a brilliant actor. He's the complete package.

Robin is white hot, but Pam Dawber is really the cement of that show. They couldn't have done better than casting her as Mindy. She's like Bud Abbott. Everybody thinks Lou Costello is great, but if there's no Bud Abbott to set him up, you've got a problem. In terms of Robin and Pam, very few women could handle it the way she does. She's calm and cool and she waits him out. Robin goes on the rampage and starts to do eight minutes of something that has nothing to do with the show. Pam just waits. As soon as she finds an opening, she sets him up for the next line and they get back on track. Pam never really gets the credit that's due her, which is terribly unfair. Robin loves Pam and respects her, and she has the same feeling about him. It's mutual respect, not a love affair. Pam has a great comic sense and is the perfect foil for Robin. She's instinctively good. She really understands her role on the show and I can't imagine anyone being as solid as she is.

During rehearsal one day, Robin and Pam are sitting on the couch. I say, "Robin, you've got to get up and make a cross here."

He says, "I can't, Papa." (Robin calls me "Papa" because at the time, I have a beard and moustache and I remind him of Ernest "Papa" Hemingway.) I ask, "What do you mean?" Robin says, "Lumpy's acting up." He stands up and he has an erection that pushes the front of his khaki pants *way* out – and I don't think he's wearing underwear. Without saying a word, Pam walks into the kitchen, grabs a saucepan, walks back to the couch and hangs it on his dick. Another time, Pam opens the armoire and Robin is inside, taking a shower. He's supposed to have a towel wrapped around him, but when she opens the door, he's facing her, totally naked. She just says, "WOW!!!" and slams it shut, totally unfazed. On one show, Robin ad-libs to Pam, "Don't worry. Someday you'll have a show of your own and you won't *need* me." After the scene, she walks backstage and tells him, "Don't you ever do that again." She really snaps Robin's head off and he's shocked by how assertive she can be.

During the first season, while he's married to his first wife, Valerie, Robin is dating Pam Dawber's best friend. It's a big love affair. Word gets to us: "Valerie just drove onto the lot." We tell Robin, "Hide the girl" and we have to get her out before Valerie gets there. It's nuts.

Just as Pam Dawber doesn't get enough credit, the show's writers are underappreciated. People assume the script just says, "Robin does his thing" and then Robin makes stuff up for a half-hour. That's hardly the case. The writers work very closely with us to make the show happen. They come up with truly brilliant stuff. During rehearsal, if there's a problem, we call the writers, we tell them what the situation is, and they figure it out. In one episode, we have a scene where Robin plays poker with four other people and he plays all five characters himself. During rehearsal, I realize the scene is too much for the audience to absorb. With only two and a half minutes, it's difficult to remember which character is which, so I suggest to Robin that instead of a poker game with five players, we do a chess game in the park between an old Jew and a WASP. Robin says, "Yeah, that might work better." I call the writers and tell them my idea. They rewrite the piece and, of course, Robin adds his own stuff. It works. That's the way we function on that show.

Each week, the writers come up with wonderful material. In one episode, Mork presides over the make-believe marriage of the little black kid, played by Jeffrey Jacquet, and a little girl. It's hilariously funny. He tells them he has the power to marry them because he comes from Ork. They're about eight and nine years old.

April Kelly writes a wonderful show called "Old Fears" in which Elizabeth Kerr, who plays Mindy's grandmother, complains that all her friends are dying. Mork hears this and turns himself into an old man, so she can have company. Robin's old man is fascinating to watch. The two of them talking together is just so lovely, just so sweet and warm. At the end of the piece, she tells Mork that she knew it was him all along. During rehearsal, Elizabeth is walking away from the music store and Robin takes his cane and gooses her. He has the ability to get away with things that nobody else could do. I think, "If I did that, one of the grips would walk over, punch me in the face and say, 'Hey! You can't do that to that old woman!'" Somehow, if Robin does it, it isn't salacious. I expect Elizabeth to say, "How dare you!" but instead, it's just a dismissive "Oh, Robin..."

Every now and again, we have a problem with the censors, known in television as Standards & Practices. They often ask Robin to come in and rerecord something and replace it with a safer word or phrase. In one episode, Robin says, "Bullpucky!" We get word from the censors in New York that Robin *cannot* say "bullpucky," even though the word doesn't exist! We all get on the phone with the censor and ask why he can't say "bullpucky." This poor guy, whose job depends on protecting the network, has three or four different people talking to him at the same time. We ask, "How about 'bullshit'?" He says, "Are you kidding? That's worse than 'bullpucky'!" We keep throwing things at him: "What about 'feline pucky'?" No matter what, the censor keeps saying, "No, no, you can't!" Finally, one of the writers asks "How about 'bovine residue'?" The censor says, "Well... okay. That'll work." We all look at each other, because we're putting him on. No matter what we say, he says we can't use it – but then he okays "bovine residue"! TV is a crazy business.

When Robin branches out into feature films, it's like magic. Whatever he does, he does full out. The first film he does where he really has something to do is *The World According to Garp* and he's wonderful in it. I never see him do anything bad. He may be in some movies that aren't very good because of the material, but *he's* never bad.

When he does *Moscow on the Hudson*, he learns to play the tenor saxophone and he plays it in the film. He also learns to speak Russian. That's not easy, to learn a language and learn an instrument just for a film, but he does it. Paul Mazursky, who directs it, is absolutely stunned by what Robin can do.

For *Popeye*, Robin learns how to tumble. I'm on the set for that, because I bring legendary acrobat Lou Wills to teach Robin tumbling. I'd studied with Lou years earlier. I'm in a room with a mat set up and Lou is teaching Robin how to do flips and somersaults. It took me years to get it right. Robin gets it in about three weeks.

Good Morning, Vietnam is perfect for Robin. It couldn't be a better fit: A guy doing a radio show and talking off the top of his head. It's based on a guy that really did that, but not as good as Robin does it. *Good Will Hunting* and *Dead Poets Society* are two more solid films for Robin.

I'm so impressed with Robin's range and versatility, that at the end of the first season, I try to get the screen rights to *Catcher in the Rye*, because I think Robin would be perfect as Holden Caulfield. J.D. Salinger won't budge. As a matter of fact, we can't even get to him to get officially turned down. It would've been a brilliant movie, and Robin was young enough then to play a seventeen-year-old and get away with it. We'll never know how that might've turned out.

Gary Nardino is the head of Paramount Television when I'm doing *Mork & Mindy*. The second year of the show, he makes a "housekeeping deal" with me, which means I get an office, a secretary and Paramount has the right of first refusal on any ideas I have. I do thirty-one shows that year and because of all the money they're paying out, they really want to get their money's worth out of me. At the end of the year, there's still $35,000 left on the contract. I call Gary and tell him, "You owe me $35,000. It feels weird taking it without working for it. Why don't you lend me out to a studio to do a pilot?" He says, "I can't do that. If you do a pilot for another studio and the show becomes a major hit, I'm gonna look like a fool. I'd rather give you the thirty-five thou," which he does.

The housekeeping deal doesn't start till June. My agent calls me in May and says, "They want you to shoot a couple of screen tests for a thousand dollars apiece." They're trying to find a guy to play the part eventually played by Judd Hirsch on *Taxi*. My agent says, "They want to take the money out of the money you're guaranteed." I tell him, "Wait a minute. My contract doesn't start till June, so they have to pay me for this." There's a big brouhaha – over two thousand dollars. I'm on the *Mork & Mindy* set and I get a phone call from Gary Nardino: "Come up to my office. I want to talk to you." I go up to his office. Gary's a big, heavyset Italian guy, like a Mafioso, with a button under his desk that closes and locks the door when he steps on it. He says, "What's going on with you, you little *pisher?* You're gonna hold me up for a couple of thousand dollars?" I tell him, "I'm not holding you up. It's only fair. My contract doesn't start until June. You're asking me to do some work in May, so I should get paid for it." Gary says, "Okay, tell your agent that I'm gonna buy you a gift." I ask, "What's the gift?" He says, "No gift. Just tell your agent that and then do the screen tests." I tell him, "You're asking me to *lie* to my agent and I'm still not getting what I should be getting." Every time Cindy Williams or Penny Marshall holds out, Gary says, "What do you need?" Cindy says, "A washing machine." He sends a washing machine. Penny says, "A refrigerator." He sends a refrigerator. Then they come back to work. It's a silly game. Gary says, "Okay, I'll buy you a gift. What do you want?" I tell him, "I want a Blaupunkt stereo for my Mercedes." He says, "Okay, you got it. Tell your agent everything's fine." I agree to shoot the tests.

I'm back on the *Mork & Mindy* set and I get a call from Nardino: "You little sonofabitch! Do you know how much that Blaupunkt costs?" I say, "Yes, seven hundred and fifty dollars." He says, "*That's* the gift you want me to pay for? I'm not buying you a Blaupunkt! I'll pay you for the tests." I tell him, "Okay." So he pays me the two thousand dollars rather than buying me the $750 Blaupunkt! It's all about control with those guys.

If I were running a series, I would have one director, because he gets to know the show, the characters and the situations, and it becomes easy. If you come in and do two episodes and you're gone and then somebody else comes in and does three, it's not cohesive. I think the reason that they seldom have one director on a show now is that they don't want him to get too much power. On *Mork & Mindy*, I have the power. Robin likes me and he wants me there. It gets to a point where I get a call at ten o'clock at night from the writers asking, "You think you can get Robin to say this?" I say, "Sure. Not a problem." They know there are things they can't get him to do that I can.

During *Mork & Mindy*, my dad is about ninety and he asks me one day, "What does a director do?" I walk him through the entire week. My dad says, "So you're a big shot." I ask, "What do you mean, Pop?" He says, "Well, they hire you to do all the big shows, so you're a big shot." I smile and say, "Okay, Pop. I'm a big shot." It's very gratifying hearing this, after years of him thinking I wasn't funny and worrying about how I'm going to make a living. I suspect there was always some envy with my father during my standup days, but now that I'm a director, there's no competition and he's freer to be happy for me without feeling jealous.

On the other hand, my mother is *always* in my corner, even in my struggling standup days. When I go with Rollins, she's very excited for me. She always tells me that I'm worth having the best and being the best.

CHAPTER TWENTY-THREE

During the second season, Robin starts refusing to say the popular catchphrases "Na-Nu Na-Nu" and "Shazbot." I ask him why and he says, "Because the character should've grown by now." I tell him, "Robin, if Archie Bunker grows, you don't have a show. If you're really concerned about that, then just use it sparingly. English is a second language to Mork. Your first language is Ork. So when you're excited, you might fall back into your first language, and when you're around Mindy, you're relaxed enough to use those phrases." I can't get him to do it. I can't get Buddy Morra to talk him into it. I can't get Garry Marshall to talk to him about it. The show starts to become about a funny guy in Boulder who's doing coke and tossing in a lot of political material.

There are plenty of changes the second season that *aren't* Robin's doing. ABC changes the day it airs from Thursday to Sunday, because they want to knock off *All in the Family*, which is crazy. *All in the Family* has its audience, which is not interested in *Mork & Mindy*. *Mork & Mindy* has its audience, a much younger audience, and we aren't competing with *All in the Family* and shouldn't be competing with them. They also get rid of Conrad Janis, as Pam's father, and Elizabeth Kerr. Their argument is, "We want to bring in people more Robin's and Pam's age, so let's get rid of the older characters." Also gone is the little black kid, Jeffrey Jacquet, who's adorable on the show. Robin has a great rapport with him. Whenever he enters, Robin says, "Hey, my main Munchkin!" and they do this elaborate handshake and dance and bump hips. The audience loves it, but they decide he's not coming back.

They also get rid of Conrad Janis' music store and they bring in two wonderful actors, Jay Thomas and Gina Hecht, as a brother and sister from New York who move to Boulder and buy a luncheonette. They're very good, but every show in the world has a luncheonette or coffee shop. The music store was so much more interesting and it gave us the chance to let Conrad Janis play his trombone. Conrad is only gone one season, because they realize they've made a mistake. They ask him back for the third season and he tells them, "If you want me back, I want a *lot* more money." He gets it. But they don't bring back Elizabeth Kerr or Jeffrey Jacquet. One *positive* addition to the second season is Tom Poston. Before Conrad Janis was cast, Tom had been our original choice to play Pam's father, but the network wouldn't agree to it. Tom plays Mr. Bickley, the upstairs neighbor, who is a pilot and an alcoholic. He always comes downstairs with the miniature liquor bottles that you get on airplanes and he drinks out of them throughout the scene. It's a funny image and a funny idea and Tom does a really great drunk.

In a particularly memorable episode from Season Two, Mork comes home and tells Mindy he just met this great group of people who are going to clean up Boulder. He says, "We're getting rid of the spics and the kikes and the coloreds!" Obviously, this is a group of people who are outrageously prejudiced and a big problem. Mindy is shocked and explains, "These are *not* nice people, Mork. They're talking about Spanish people, Jewish people and black people that they want to get out of Boulder." Mork decides that when he goes to the meeting, he's going to zap them and turn them all different colors. We have the KKK meeting and we see all white rednecks. They put their hoods on and while the Grand Master is speaking, Mork zaps them. I have Robin find a place to screw up intentionally so I have to yell, "Cut!" We have a second group of people backstage with hoods on. We tell all the white actors to casually stroll offstage at some point, just as someone else is strolling on. Before you know it, we've replaced all the people onstage. I say, "Okay, we're ready to go!" The meeting ends, the KKK members take off their hoods and it's a black guy, an American Indian, a Chinese guy, a Spanish guy! The audience is absolutely stunned. They can't figure out how it happened. They're standing there, Mork zaps them, and now they're all changed! I love that we're able to fool them with that little trick.

During the second season, ABC feels the show needs some tits and ass, so they hire Raquel Welch for a two-parter. She plays

Captain Nirvana, a woman from another planet who's come to kidnap Robin. She has two female lieutenants. One is played by an actress named Vicki Frederick, who starred in *Dancin'* and *Chorus Line* on Broadway. She's a real trouper – solid, tough, very attractive, great figure. The other is played by Debra Jo Fondren from Texas, the current Playmate of the Year. She has a terrific figure and thick blonde hair that goes down to her ankles. The first day, we do the read-through. Raquel is on my right and the two girls are on her right. After the read-through, we dismiss everybody but the star and then we ask, "Do you have any questions?" Present are Bruce Johnson and Dale McRaven, who are the Exec Producers, Garry Marshall, Pam Dawber, Robin, Raquel and me. Raquel says, "Yes. Who are the girls that are going to play my lieutenants?" I tell her, "The two girls who just read with you." She says, "Oh, I didn't notice them." I ask, "Anything else, Raquel?" She says, "Yes, my entrance doesn't work. They can't come in before me. I have to come in first." I tell her, "But Raquel, if you come in first and they come in after you, they're gonna pull the eye away from you. The idea is that one girl comes in, walks downstage left, poses, and the audience knows that's not you. There's anticipation. The other girl comes in, walks downstage right, poses. No, that's not you. And then *you* enter and you're center stage and there you are, flanked by your two lieutenants!" Raquel says, "No, they can't come in before me, but I have an idea. Supposing they wear dog masks and I lead them in on leashes."

While we're rehearsing, she's *still* pushing for dog masks, but we're not going to do it. Robin tells her, "The entrance is really good as it stands. It's exciting." Robin tries to convince Raquel to leave the entrance the way it is and Raquel tells him no. Pam says, "Y'know, Raquel, Robin is right." Raquel steps in front of Pam, saying, "Honey, please..." Then she turns her back on Pam and continues talking to Robin. Pam pantomimes that she's going to bash in the back of Raquel's head. After that, every time Raquel comes onstage, Pam goes behind her back and makes like she's going to bop her on the head.

Raquel has her fiancé with her, a Frenchman named Andre Weinfeld who has worked in French TV. He stands behind me and every time I give her a note, I see her look past me to see what Andre thinks. After awhile, I start to spin around real fast to catch him giving her either a nod or a shake of the head. One day, I tell her, "Raquel, I need you a little closer to Robin for the two-shot. You realize that's one of the most brilliant notes a director has ever given an actress." She says, "What are you talking about?" I say, "I know it's great, because Andre agreed with me," and I walk away. The fight ends in a split decision: Raquel gets to make her entrance before the two girls, but we nix the dog masks.

My friend from the Betty Garrett experience, Marty Nedboy, really loves show business. He's funny and talented, but frightened to death. He just can't bring that talent onstage. I get him a job on *Mork & Mindy* holding book, which means he prompts actors who forget a line and is available if an actor wants to run lines before shooting. I tell Garry Marshall, "We need a guy to hold book for the cast. I have the perfect guy." Thank God Garry doesn't ask, "What's this guy done before?" because Marty's never done anything in television before. Garry says, "We only have three hundred dollars." I tell him, "That's fine," and Marty takes the job.

Then Frank Pace, a producer, falls in love with Marty and keeps him working. Marty starts to get ill and has dizzy spells, so Frank sends a car for him. They pick him up and bring him to work like he's a star. He's only able to come in around eleven and then leave at three, because of his dizzy spells. Frank tells me, "He comes in, goes straight to the craft-service table, stuffs his face with food, and leaves." He calls Marty "America's Guest." Frank hires Marty for *Suddenly Susan* and *The George Lopez Show*. Every now and again, they use Marty to play bit parts, like an elevator operator, so Frank gets him a SAG contract. That means he's getting a health plan and a retirement fund. *The George Lopez Show* is sold into syndication and Marty gets residuals for every episode. Sadly, he dies not long after that, but he's well taken care of in his later years.

David Huddleston, a wonderful actor, is playing a mayor in a sitcom called *Hizzoner*, which he created with Sheldon Keller. He comes to the set of *Mork & Mindy* and tells me, "You've *got* to do my show!" I say, "David, I don't have time. I'm doing *Mork & Mindy*." He says, "You get a week or two off sometimes. Can't you do it then?" I think about it and then I tell him, "Okay." During a break in *Mork & Mindy*, I direct an episode of *Hizzoner*. David's a terrific actor, but as a producer, he dictates everything. Even though I'm directing, he's telling everyone, "Don't pay any attention to him. Talk to *me*." I see him take one actor aside and say, "Whatever it is, check with me first." David has a habit of constantly goosing his lovely co-star, Diana Muldaur. One day, I walk up to her and I ask, "Would you like me to talk to him about the goosing and tell him to stop it?" She says, "No, I can handle that. Just tell him to stop *directing* me!" When I give him notes, I say, "David, when you make that cross, I..." and he cuts me off with a dismissive, "Yeah-yeah-yeah." Every time I give him a note: "Yeah-yeah-yeah." I take him aside and I say, "David, listen, you can't 'yeah-yeah-yeah' me. Either you don't want the notes – and that's fine with me – or I'll give you notes privately. But don't *ever* do that again in front of the rest of the cast, because I will fuckin' *bury* you right in front of the cast." He looks at me, puzzled: "What do you mean?" I tell him, "*You* know what." He says, "Yeah-yeah-yeah, okay."

On Friday night, we're shooting the show and David can't remember a word of the script. I say, "Cut." Because the show is being taped, I'm in the booth, rather than down on the set. Through the headset, the stage manager says to me, "David wants to know why we're doing a pickup." I don't want to embarrass David, so I say, "Tell him we had a technical problem." This goes on and on, with David flubbing his lines, me having to cut, and the stage manager telling me, "David wants to know why we're stopping and redoing that shot." Each time, I say, "Tell him it's a technical problem." The fourth time we go through this, David turns to the audience and he's ready to strangle somebody because of all these "technical problems." We finally get through the show and then the next morning, my phone rings: "Howard?! David! What *happened* last night?! Why were there so many technical problems?!" I tell him, "You fat tub of shit! How *dare* you call me on a Saturday morning and ask me why there were technical problems! Are you fuckin' kidding me? You didn't know a word of the show. I'm trying to protect you and not embarrass you, so I'm saying it's a technical problem, and now you're asking me why there were so many technical problems?!? I don't want my option picked up. I want a meeting Monday morning and I want out of the show." I get to the studio Monday and David appears with his lawyer! David asks, "What *really* went on last Friday?" Before I can say a word, Sheldon Keller, the producer, says, "David, you fucking idiot! You didn't know a word of the script! He's trying to protect you and you're demanding to know about *technical problems*? *You* were the problem! You didn't know one goddamn word!" That ends the meeting and to my great relief, my option is not picked up. NBC is actually hoping that *Hizzoner* will bury *Mork & Mindy* in the ratings. Boy, are they ever wrong.

In and around my *Mork & Mindy* responsibilities, I direct a few episodes of *Too Close For Comfort*. That's a lot of fun. I love Ted Knight. He's a real good guy and, of course, very funny. I actually worked with Ted a few years earlier when I directed a few episodes of *The Ted Knight Show*, in which he played a retired guy who runs an escort service. That show didn't make it, but *Too Close For Comfort* is a hit. Ted and I spend a lot of time together, especially at a restaurant near KTLA, where we're shooting. We refer to the restaurant as The Women's Auxiliary, because it's very old fashioned and there are a lot of blue-haired ladies. One time, the waiter comes up and says, "The special today is Chicken Valentino." Ted asks, "What's Chicken Valentino?" I tell him, "It's a chicken with its feathers slicked back."

Another time, Ted and I have lunch at a Japanese restaurant in Gower Gulch. We leave in his Jaguar and traffic is really heavy, so we're sitting in the driveway, waiting to turn. Two black guys are walking towards us with giant smiles on their faces. Ted tells me, "Black guys *really* like me." The guys get close to the car and say, "Hey, Howie! How are ya? What's happenin'?" They're two grips that I'd worked with on another show. I tell Ted, "Black guys may like you, but they *love* me."

CHAPTER TWENTY-FOUR

A lot of *Mork & Mindy* fans have fond memories of Robin's idol, Jonathan Winters, playing Mork and Mindy's son, Mearth. That character doesn't appear until the fourth season, after I leave the show, but I do get to work with Johnny in a third-season episode where he's cast as Mindy's uncle, Dave McConnell, who is a billionaire and an asshole. Robin pushes hard to bring Johnny in and he's so excited when Johnny shows up. They start talking and playing off each other and it's a delight to watch. But I also hear Johnny zing Robin a little bit. As much as Robin adores Johnny and tells everyone that Jonathan Winters is his idol and inspiration, Johnny resents Robin's success: This young kid is in awe of me and now, all of a sudden, he's getting me a job.

The comparison between Robin and Johnny is an understandable one because they're both brilliant improvisers, but Johnny's brilliance is all out of Ohio, where Johnny was born. Most of his characters are small-town people – Maude Frickert and Elwood P. Suggins and all those military men. Robin has a much larger frame of reference. Also, Johnny is not really a great actor, while Robin is a wonderful, versatile actor. Robin can do everything that Johnny can, and so much more. You always see that clip from *The Jack Paar Show* where Paar gives Johnny a stick and he does a bunch of things with it off the top of his head. Robin does the same thing with a shawl on *Inside the Actor's Studio*. Robin's reference base is like a panorama. Johnny's brilliant, of course. You can throw Johnny a rose and he can do ten minutes on that rose, but Robin might do it as Shakespeare, while Johnny does it as a guy from Ohio.

I like working with Johnny. He's very sweet and also very crazy. One day, I walk into the green room and he's talking to a guy in a chair who isn't there. He's in there alone, talking to the guy for five minutes before I come in. He's telling an empty chair, "Sergeant! You'll be brought up on charges!" I walk in and he says, "Ah, Colonel! I'm glad you're here. Tell the Sergeant why he's being brought up on charges!" and he pulls me into doing an improv that I really have no time for. In the first scene of Johnny's episode, Mindy hasn't seen Uncle Dave in years. When he's reintroduced to Mindy, his first line is an innocent, "My how you've grown." But when we're doing it, Johnny looks her up and down salaciously and says, "My, my...how you've *grown...*" I tell him, "John, you can't do that! This is your *niece*. You have to say the line straight. You haven't seen her since she was four years old and she's all grown up now." We finally get what we need.

There's another incident during the shooting of that show where a joke depends on Johnny saying the word "coffee," but he keeps saying, "I'd love some Java" or "I'd love a cup of Joe" or "I'd love something caffeinated." He decides the word "coffee" is never going to be uttered. I tell him, "John, I'm going to get cue cards and I'm going to put a camera on you and I want you to read every line from the cue cards. Then tonight, you can do whatever you want. Okay? Is that fair?" He's cool with that. No matter what he does in front of the audience, we're covered.

In the story, Mork drops a pill into Johnny's drink, he drinks it and goes nuts. He starts doing scenes from every war from the American Revolution on. He's a Confederate soldier, then he's riding a horse up San Juan Hill, then he's a doughboy in the First World War and a G.I. in the Second World War. That one piece, as Johnny plays it, runs twenty-two minutes, which is the length of an entire episode, minus commercials. It would be lovely to have an hour show and allow Johnny to do that whole piece, but I can't do that, so I have to find cutaways from Johnny so we can trim the scene to a manageable length. I cut to Pam reacting, to Robin reacting, to ashtrays, a lamp – anything to cut away from Johnny's rambling manifesto. Finally, the scene winds up being about seven minutes long. At one point, I witness true brilliance. Johnny is behind the couch with an imaginary machine gun and he's firing away. Robin is on his right feeding him the belt with all the bullets. Suddenly, Johnny decides the gun has jammed and Robin senses it at the exact same moment. When Johnny pantomimes that the gun has jammed, Robin instantly yells, "Ow!" and pretends he got his finger caught in the firing mechanism. That's how in tune they are.

During the third season, Robin's problem with coke worsens. Once the show becomes hot, all the stars want to hang out with this brilliant, young, new performer. He's invited to every A-list party and there's loads of coke just sitting there. I try it once or twice and I don't like it, but Robin gets into it in a big way. Also, Robin is screwing every woman in the city. To keep him close to Paramount, they get him an apartment in The Ravenswood – Mae West's apartment building in Hollywood. We call there, no answer. We call all over the city trying to find him. He shows up an hour and a half late and there's always an excuse: "The cab broke down" or "I couldn't get a cab" or "My car broke down." To come down from the coke high, people drink booze, so Robin's on vodka and coke and it's a very sad thing to watch. Robin comes to the set and we rehearse awhile and then we take a break for five minutes and we can't find him. He's either in a cupboard or under the bleachers. He finds a place to hide so he can grab five minutes of sleep. He's exhausted. He's burning the candle at both ends and I really believe his later heart attack is due to the coke. There's something about that insidious substance that people just love.

Robin is still able to hit his mark and entertain the studio audience, but he's no longer playing full out. I tell him, "Robin, you're so good that the audience accepts seventy-five percent, but I know you're not giving me a hundred percent. Your work is getting mediocre and my work is getting mediocre. If you're not willing to come in here and give a hundred percent, I'm going to leave." He says, "No, no, Papa! Don't do it! I'll be good!" But really, by that time, he's just phoning it in – and he's so good, he can get away with it. With most performers, the audience would notice, but Robin at seventy-five percent is still so much more than what others would give full out. As Robin's coke problem worsens, it becomes more difficult to interact with him creatively. I go to the green room to give him notes and he's lying down. I don't know if he's awake or asleep. I feel foolish leaning over somebody, talking to them, and their eyes are closed. I ask, "Robin, did you hear me?" I get nothing. I kick him in the shoulder. He wakes up and I tell him, "Robin, I need you to do such-and-such." He says, "Okay, Papa, okay." This happens with increasing frequency. Finally, I tell him, "Robin, I can't do this anymore, leaning over and kicking you in the shoulder to give you notes. Either you take the notes sitting up and awake or I'll give you private notes or whatever you want, but you can't do this. It's uncomfortable for me to be talking to somebody while trying to figure out whether they're hearing me or not."

In the meantime, I'm offered seventeen episodes on *Taxi* and I figure that will be a nice change. I also believe I'll finally have a shot at getting an Emmy. As brilliant as *Mork & Mindy* is, it's viewed as little more than a children's show and the misconception is that all I really do is "turn Robin loose." I tell Garry Marshall, "I'm getting a little burned out on *Mork & Mindy*, having directed fifty-nine episodes. I've been offered *Taxi*. Are you okay with me taking that?" I'm not going to accept the *Taxi* job and then tell Garry about it after the fact. I want his blessing, because he's been very good to me. To my relief, he's fine with my leaving the show.

I'm excited about the job on *Taxi*, but I'm sad about leaving *Mork & Mindy*, because I love Robin and I love working with him and with Pam. Years later, she tells me, "You were the only director that Robin respected, because you weren't intimidated by him. Every time you left and someone else came in, it was a problem." As nice a guy as Robin is, when a director is not controlling the scene, the actor will eat him up alive. From what I hear, Robin has trouble with a lot of the directors who follow me. A couple of years after I leave the show, Robin's with Robert De Niro and John Belushi at the Chateau Marmont. They leave John and about twenty minutes later, they hear that Belushi has overdosed. It scares the hell out of Robin and he backs off of the coke – for a while. But he has an addictive personality. He cleans up for a long time, but somehow, he gets sucked in again and he goes back into rehab. It's terribly sad to hear about. In later years, I don't see much of Robin. In 1991, I'm invited to his 40th birthday party at his house up in Napa Valley. I also see him once or twice at concerts where he's performing. Backstage, after one of the concerts, he tells my wife, Patricia, "He used to give me notes by kicking me in the shoulder."

His suicide in 2014 is a terrible shock. It's just so very sad. There will never be another Robin Williams. Of all the performers I've seen – the brilliance of a guy like Jonathan Winters, the brilliance of Sid Caesar, Jackie Gleason – he outshines *all* of them, because he was a better *actor* than any of them. The things that came out of his head were just incredible. I believe he was a savant; that he was born with that somehow. He'd remember things from forty years earlier or he'd quote from a book. Unlike someone like Dennis Miller, he didn't do it to show you how smart he was. There was always a sweetness about him.

CHAPTER TWENTY-FIVE

In 1981, I'm set to do seventeen episodes of *Taxi* and I'm really looking forward to it, but it doesn't work out quite the way I'd hoped. Director Jim Burrows leaves *Taxi* to do the movie, *Partners*. I'm watching my son play baseball in Roxbury Park and I run into Jim Burrows' brother-in-law, Peter Grad. He asks, "How are you doing?" I tell him, "Fine. How's Jim?" He says, "Jim's doing great. He's coming back to do *Taxi*." I call my agent and I tell him, "Peter Grad tells me that Jim is doing *Taxi*. What's goin' on?" He calls me back and says, "Yeah, Jim's coming back. They want to split the shows with you, nine each." I tell him, "Wait a minute. I had seventeen! Tell them to pay me off!" He says, "No, don't do that. You'll get them upset." They tell me Jim will do the first nine, but with the season about to start, that means I'll have nothing going on until my nine shows come up. I tell producer Ed. Weinberger, "The reality is, Jim won't be able to do all those shows, because he's editing his film. I will bet you that he doesn't do three or four of them. So what I want is a guarantee that if he doesn't do a show, it's mine, in addition to the nine they're offering me."

Jim's agent calls my agent and says, "Jim will switch. When he can't do it, he'll switch with Howard." I tell my agent, "Elliott, that's crazy! What am I, standing in the wings waiting for Jim to make up his mind if he's going to do it and then I give up a show and he gets that? No! I won't switch with him, but I'll tell you what I *will* do: Tell him I'll switch all nine. I'll do the first nine and by then, he'll be finished editing his movie and he can do the second nine." No – he has to control it. We agree to the 9/9 and there's a party at Ed. Weinberger's house. Jim comes up to me and asks, "How come you wouldn't switch shows with me?" I tell him, "Jim, you've got a lot of goddamn nerve! I'm doing seventeen shows, you decide you're coming back and knock me out of the box, and then you want me to sit around and wait for you to decide what shows you can and can't do?" He says, "I didn't know you were doing seventeen." I tell him, "You gotta be kidding me. You leave a show and you don't know who replaced you? It was in *Variety*. I mean, it was a big deal."

I shoot my first *Taxi*. Judd Hirsch and Danny DeVito are a little standoffish. I figure it's because I'm a new director and they're used to Jim. Marilu Henner, on the other hand, is very sweet and very open. Jim Burrows is on the stage, standing with the producers. I see them whispering and talking about a particular shot. In the scene, Danny is on the steps leading up to the cage where he works and he sees something that makes him faint and fall backwards. We're not really going to let him fall backwards onto his office floor, but if I shoot it head on, we'll see the mattress he falls on, so I shoot him in profile and we see him disappear out of frame. Jim's telling them to shoot it the other way, which would reveal the mattress. I tell him, "You can't shoot it that way. You're going to see the mattress. If you can find a way to hide it, fine, but if not, he's gotta just fall out of frame."

Andy Kaufman is a sweet man. He's very humble, almost like Tiny Tim calling everybody "Mister" and "Miss" – except with Tim, it seemed like part of his act, but with Andy, it's genuine. He's very low-key, very respectful, very easy to talk with. Andy doesn't seem comfortable in his own skin, so he hides behind all these characters, but when you have a conversation with him, he seems extremely normal. And, of course, he's extremely talented. The episode I do that features Andy is called "Mr. Personalities." In it, he "becomes" Judd Hirsch's character, Alex. It's just brilliant. I mean, he *is* Judd Hirsch. He starts to dress like Alex dresses and is talking and acting like Alex and it's driving Alex crazy. I find out that Andy doesn't come to rehearsals; he only shows up on shoot day, which is really outrageous to me. Barry Nelson is playing the psychiatrist that Andy goes to see, but during rehearsal, there's an extra on the set reading Andy's lines. On shoot day, when Andy comes in, the extra shows him the marks. I'm thinking, as an actor, I don't want to work with an extra in rehearsal. When you have the real actor there, there's a completely different tone and tempo than you'd have with a stand-in. I apologize to Barry Nelson, who is a professional and a respected veteran of Broadway, movies and TV. I tell him, "Mr.

Nelson, I really feel terrible. I had no idea that this was happening. I know it's difficult for you to work off someone who's not the actual actor that you're going to work with." He tells me, "It's okay. Don't worry about it." He's really a gentleman about the whole thing.

Andy has other idiosyncrasies that interfere with the production of the show. You can't shoot until Andy finishes meditating, which is crazy, because if his meditation goes on for an hour, you're holding the show up until he finishes. Andy has two contracts, one for him and one for his obnoxious alter ego, Tony Clifton. He has two dressing rooms, one for him and one for Tony Clifton. He has two parking spaces, one for him and one for Tony Clifton. At one point, Tony Clifton isn't working out, so the producers tell Andy, "We're going to have to get rid of the Tony Clifton character. It doesn't work." Andy says, "Oh, okay." A half-hour later, Tony Clifton appears: "Nobody fires me! Are you fuckin' kidding me?! I fire *you*! You know who I am? I'm Tony Clifton!" Judd says, "Andy, please, stop it." Tony says, "Whaddaya mean 'Andy'?! I'm Tony Clifton! Who's Andy? I don't know any Andy!" It gets to the point where Judd wants to kill him. They get security and they walk Tony Clifton off the lot and he's not allowed on again. But you can't stop him from coming onto the lot, because Andy *is* Tony Clifton – even though he never cops to it.

I do the first two episodes of *Taxi*, because – big surprise – Jim Burrows can't do them, since he's editing his movie. I get an offer to do two episodes of *Gimme a Break*. I go to Ed. Weinberger and I tell him, "Ed, I've been offered *Gimme a Break*, but I won't take it if Jimmy's not doing the third episode. I'll do it." Ed. says, "No, no, he definitely said he's coming back for the third one." So I agree to do *Gimme a Break* and I find out that Jim can't do the third show after all, so they give it to Joan Darling. I do the first two *Taxi* episodes, Joan does the third, then Jim Burrows comes back for the fourth show. While Jim is there, my agent tells me, "We got a problem. The cast is unhappy with you." I tell him, "That's very interesting. They weren't unhappy with me for the two shows I did or for Joan Darling's show, but while Jim is there, they're suddenly unhappy with me. You know what? Tell them to pay me off. I don't want to deal with this." They make a deal with me to switch over to a series called *Best of the West* with Joel Higgins. I've already done a couple of episodes – which is what led to my being offered *Taxi* in the first place! It's a crazy business.

Before returning to *Best of the West*, I do the two episodes of *Gimme a Break* for Mort Lachman, a very good producer and a very solid writer. Nell Carter and I have a great time working together. She calls me "the Little White Director." My Stage Manager is a nice-looking Italian kid. One day, Nell invites me into her dressing room and says, "Will you send in that young Stage Manager?" It's very clear that she'd like to screw him. I tell her, "When you buy me a pink Cadillac and a purple suit, I'll pimp for you. But until then, if you want him, you go after him yourself."

Having already directed a couple of episodes of *Best of the West* for Ed. Weinberger before *Taxi*, I return to that show to do four more. Ed. is doing a lot of coke and is truly crazy. He calls me one morning at nine o'clock and asks me, "Are you in the cabin?" I tell him, "Yes, I'm rehearsing the cabin scene." He says, "Okay, here's what I want. I want a single of Joel Higgins, a single of Carlene Watkins and a single of Meeno Peluce at the end of the scene." I start to tell him, "I can't get you..." and he interrupts with, "Don't tell me you can't get me! I'm the producer! You work for me! You get me what I want!" I tell him, "Ed, I'll see you at the run-through." In the script, Meeno leaves the cabin three pages before the scene ends. I tell Ed., "Do you see what I'm talking about now? He's no longer in the scene and you can't shoot someone who isn't there." He drives me nuts.

Then we have a bank scene and the holdup, but the bank has been designed very ornately, with a lot of heavy wrought-iron all over the place, which makes filming difficult and throws shadows over everyone. I tell Ed., "The set looks beautiful, but you're going to have everybody in shadow because of all the iron grill work." Ed. says, "You're always complaining you can't get this, you can't get that." I tell him, "Fine. Whatever you want." Later, Ed. tells me, "Everybody's *blocked*! You can't see them! Get rid of all that wrought-iron stuff!" So we get rid of it.

I need a quick pickup of Dixie Carter. We get the shot at the end of the show because otherwise, makeup has to come and start doing

Dixie's makeup again, hair has to do her hair, and she'd have to sit for thirty-five minutes. Ed. comes screaming at me while the audience is sitting there. "What did you do? You don't do a pickup with an audience!" I say, "What are you talking about, Ed.? We do pickups with the audience all the time." He screams, "You ruined the show! You ruined the show by doing that pickup!" I tell him, "You know what? You're the producer. You're not happy, do something about it." He says, "Maybe you shouldn't come in tomorrow." I tell him, "Ed., you're an Executive Producer. You have to be decisive. 'Maybe'? You've gotta say yes or no." I *want* him to fire me so I can get the money, because if I quit, I don't get paid. Finally, he says, "You're fired!" I tell him, "Thank you." He walks away and that's the end of it, because I already have the shot. It costs them $45,000 to pay me off for the rest of my contract.

I direct the pilot of *Madame's Place*, starring Wayland Flowers and his puppet, Madame. Every time I give a note to Wayland, Madame answers! Even when I'm just talking to Wayland and not giving notes, Madame is the one who replies. I develop a newfound respect for the no-nonsense way Jules Podell handled Velvel at the Copa. I am not going to direct an entire episode of a show while talking to Madame instead of Wayland. Whenever Madame starts to answer, I lock eyes with Wayland and refuse to look at the puppet, but Madame keeps providing the answers. One day, a pouting Wayland asks me, "How come you won't ever talk to Madame?" I tell him, "Because Madame is a fuckin' *dummy*, that's why!" It makes no difference. Wayland will only talk to me through Madame. In one scene, we're doing a takeoff on Julia Child. Wayland is sitting on the floor behind the kitchen counter. He's got a script and a small TV monitor next to him so he can see what's going on. Wayland has Madame say, "Well, you take the chicken and you stuff it, making sure to remove the giblets ahead of time." During rehearsal, I say, "Camera Two, can you give me as wide a shot as you can? I want to see the entire set." We pull back and there's a guy standing between the cameras holding cue cards – *for Madame!* I get hysterical and then the whole crew starts to crack up. Wayland can't see the cards, because he's on the floor behind the counter, so the cards are *only* for Madame! Wayland insists on having them there in case Madame goes up on her lines. That's how crazy things can get with ventriloquists.

CHAPTER TWENTY-SIX

In and around my directing adventures, I get the chance to indulge another lifelong passion, which has nothing to do with acting, directing, or standup. Just as my father would regularly take my brother Eddie and me to the fights as kids, Eddie and I go to the fights every Thursday night at the Olympic Auditorium in downtown L.A. We have ringside seats and we go constantly. One night, we meet a wonderful welterweight fighter named Armando Muniz, who had come very close to being the champ. His cousin is a bantamweight named Oscar "The Boxer" Muniz. We've seen Oscar fight a few times and he's really good. One day, Armando says, "My cousin's contract is up in January and he's looking for new management. Are you guys interested?" Eddie and I tell him, "Yes" and we take on Oscar! We have two other partners, Rocky Kalish and Alex Santana.

Oscar's former manager is a good one, but he's been pushing Oscar to the sidelines and focusing on some of the other, higher-profile fighters in his weight class. Apart from our longtime passion, Eddie and I have no real training in managing a boxer, but we sense we can do something with Oscar, who has never made more than $13,000 in any given year. In the year we handle him, he makes $105,000. Even though Oscar has won an impressive number of fights, he never gets ranked in the top ten of his weight class by Ring Magazine. In order to get a title fight, your name *has* to be on that top-ten list. I start inundating the two big boxing associations – WBA and WBO – with wires and letters saying, "Oscar's beaten three of the fighters on your top-ten list, so why isn't he in the top ten?" Someone tells me, "I can get him on the top ten of the WBA for five thousand dollars." I say, "No, he's gonna *prove* that he's the better fighter and he'll get there on his own."

There's a big fight coming up in Vegas, so Eddie and I fly up there to meet with the president of the WBO. As he's leaving a press conference, I corner him in the hotel hallway and tell him, "I manage Oscar Muniz. I don't care if he only makes number ten on the top-ten list, but it's unreasonable that he's not even *on* the list when he's beaten three of these guys." He agrees and Oscar gets a spot on the list. Eddie and I get a call for Oscar to fight the bantamweight champ in July of 1983 at the Sands Hotel in Atlantic City. The champ's name is "Joltin'" Jeff Chandler, a black kid out of Philadelphia. Chandler has never lost a fight and he's got thirty-one wins. Oscar keeps saying, "I want to fight Chandler." We accept the challenge and we get Oscar $20,000 for the fight.

The day of the fight, I run into Teddy Brenner, who is Bob Arum's top boxing "matchmaker" for Madison Square Garden. He tells me, "Your kid doesn't have a chance." I say, "I'll talk to you tomorrow, Teddy." Oscar fights Chandler at the Sands and he beats him. It's a split decision, but he beats him – and on ABC television. Eddie and I are exuberant over Oscar's win. We jump up and rush over to hug our boy and pat him on the back. Then Eddie tells me, "I think we need to go to the hospital." I figure he's concerned about the cuts Oscar received during the bout, so I tell him to let Oscar relax for a few minutes and then we can take him. Eddie says, "No, it's me that has to get to the hospital. It's my ankle!" In his enthusiasm, my brother jumped up and landed wrong, breaking his ankle!

The fight's promoter is a very nice guy out of Philadelphia named Russell Peltz. Nobody had ever beaten Chandler before, so ABC says they will buy a title fight between Oscar and Chandler – a rematch in December. Peltz says he'll fly out to California to meet with us about the title fight. Since he's making the effort to fly out to L.A., Eddie and I figure we must have the upper hand. Peltz flies out and we meet him for lunch at his hotel. He asks, "What do you guys want for the fight?" We know Chandler is getting $200,000 a fight, because he's the champ and he's a big star. We tell him we want $100,000. At that point, no one has ever gotten more than $40,000 to fight for the title against the champ in that weight division. Only the heavyweights get the big money. He says, "$100,000? That's crazy!" We tell him, "Well, ABC's paying a load of money and we know Jeff gets $200,000." We go back and forth and we settle on $65,000. We also say that if Oscar beats Chandler, he gets a total of $500,000 for his next three fights. That's the contract we get.

When you manage fighters, there's always *some* problem. Oscar tells us, "Everybody in the gym said I should've gotten training expenses." With training expenses, the manager doesn't get anything; it goes straight to the fighter. The guys in the gym are street kids who don't trust anybody: "Here's two Beverly Hills Jews looking to beat you for your money." I say, "Okay, Oscar. Take $5,000 off the top for training expenses and $60,000 is your fee for the fight." He's fine with that.

Oscar is worried about getting his weight down from 122 to 118 for the bantamweight bout, scheduled for December, so he stops eating. In those days, you weigh in the same day as the fight. Now you weigh in the day before. Oscar has just fought a tune-up fight at 119. I tell him, "Oscar, stay at 119 and the last couple of days, we'll get you down to 118, because one pound is not that hard to lose." We go in an hour before the weigh-in and he jumps on the scale just to see where he is. He's down to 116, so we give him a glass of orange juice. He's so dehydrated that when he drinks the orange juice, he comes up to 117. He fights later that night, but he just isn't strong. Oscar is never one to complain, but when he comes back to the corner after the first round, he says, "I'm feelin' everything he hits me with." They stop it in the seventh round because of cuts over Oscar's eyes. He isn't knocked down, but he loses the fight. As a matter of fact, in forty-eight fights, he is never knocked down.

One day, we get a visit from the father of two very good fighters – Tony "The Tiger" Baltazar and his brother, Frank – and we make a deal to manage both of them. We start handling them and then we realize the father, Frank Sr., is a problem. Eddie and I fly to New York to see Bob Arum. At that point, Tony Baltazar is not among the top ten. They have a guy named Lonnie "Lightning" Smith who *is* in the top ten and we think Tony can beat him. They also have a guy who's the champ, Greg "Mutt" Haugen, from Texas. We think he's the perfect opponent for Tony, because he comes right at you, while Tony has a great left hook. When he hits you, you go down. Both are 135-pound lightweights. The deal we make is: We'll take

$5,000 for Tony to fight Lonnie Smith, but if he beats him, we want a guarantee that he gets to fight Haugen for the title. They agree to it, which puts Tony one fight away from a title bout.

About a month before the fight with Lonnie Smith, Frank Sr. tells me, "Tony hurt his thumb during training, so he's not going to be able to fight." I tell him, "Okay, when he heals, we'll reschedule it." He says, "No, I don't want the fight." I tell him, "Frank, if he beats this kid – and I think he can – he gets a shot at the title, and I think he'll beat Haugen." Frank says, "I don't want him to fight." He doesn't explain why he feels that way. I call Teddy Brenner and I tell him, "Tony hurt his thumb. I talked to him about setting up another date for the fight after his thumb is better, but his father won't agree to it. He says he doesn't want the fight." Teddy says, "You're a nice man. What are you doing with these lowlifes?" After a few more disappointments, Frank Sr. tells us Tony wants out of his contract. We tell him, "That's fine. Just pay us the money we've put up." Frank doesn't want to pay up. I think the total is close to $16,000. We go to the Boxing Commission to arbitrate the matter. Frank tells the Commission that we promised to make Tony a movie star. What I'd told Tony was, "You're a good-looking kid. You should study acting. It couldn't hurt you. And if I can help you, I'll help you." They turned that into, "I promise to make you a movie star." He also complains that we ignore Frank Jr., but every fight that Tony has, we get Frank Jr. on that card.

In July of 1984, in what turns out to be one of his last bouts, Tony Baltazar fights Roger "Black Mamba" Mayweather, the uncle of Floyd Mayweather. Roger is very hot. He's in the top ten, unlike Tony. Nevertheless, Tony *beats* Roger Mayweather and seems to have a promising future. Unfortunately, Tony doesn't do a very good job of taking care of himself. He and a friend get coked up and go out driving. They get into an accident and the friend is killed. Tony goes to jail and we get a call that morning from Frank Jr.: "We need some money, because Tony's in jail." I tell him, "No. He was on coke. My brother and I aren't interested in bailing him out." Our relationship with the Baltazars comes to a sad end.

Eddie loses interest in boxing, but I continue to enjoy watching the sport and often stop by the gym downtown to hang out with the boxers and trainers, even though I'm no longer in the game. I'm at the gym several years later, talking to bantamweight-champ-turned-trainer Alberto Davila, when I check my answering machine and find out that Eddie has died of pancreatic cancer at the age of 64. Poor Alberto doesn't know how to handle my grief and tears, but given our lifelong love of boxing and our years together as managers, there's something bittersweet and appropriate about being at a boxing gym when I get the sad news. A week later, I'm at a boxing match at the Forum and they give Eddie a ten-count, to mark his passing. They show a giant photo of my brother and the audience stands silently while the bell chimes ten times. The announcer, Jimmy Lennon, says, "May he rest in peace." Eddie would've loved it.

CHAPTER TWENTY-SEVEN

Viacom buys the rights to do an American version of John Cleese's brilliant *Fawlty Towers* as a vehicle for the formidable Bea Arthur. They're going to call it *Amanda's By The Sea.* They've gone through five or six directors and then they bring me in. At the Monday read-through, the producer says, "Bea, this is Howard Storm. He's directing this week's show." She asks me, "Did you read the script?" I tell her, "Of course." She says, "Do you think it's funny?" I say, "Yeah." She says, "You gotta be kidding." I tell her, "Well, I don't think it's ready to shoot, but by the end of the week, we should be ready to make it work." She rolls her eyes dismissively and sits down. I'm standing there thinking, "What do I do?" I tell her, "Y'know, Miss Arthur, I have an advantage over you. I know your work and I know how good you are, but you don't know anything about me, so if you don't mind, I'd like to tell you a little about me." She says, "Okay." I tell her, "My father was a vaudevillian and a burlesque comic and I knew 'funny' at the age of two. I know what's funny and I promise you that if a joke doesn't work, I'll find a way to make it work and if I can't do that, I'll call the writers and tell them they need to write another joke. But I'll never hang you out to dry." She asks, "You promise?" and I tell her, "I promise." She says, "Okay," and from that point on, we get along famously.

The truth is, Bea isn't right for the role of a female Basil Fawlty, because she's such a sincere actress. When she says or does something, you believe it. Cleese, on the other hand, is goofy. When six-foot-four Cleese hits the little Spanish busboy in the head with a loaf of bread, you laugh because he's so goofy and it's clearly a farce. The first time in front of an audience, Bea hits the little Spanish busboy with a loaf of bread and the audience gasps. That's not the response you're hoping for. Generally speaking, Americans are not good at writing farce. We have great writers, but it's tough to do farce and Bea, being such an honest actress, doesn't help it.

Bea likes a no-nonsense set. She doesn't like to chat before a scene. If we're rehearsing, she wants to rehearse. She tells me, "One director drove me crazy, because he would sing a song to match whatever comment someone made. If they said, 'I can't get over this,' he'd turn it into a song, 'Can't get over you, I just can't get over you.'" She hates that. On my sets, we usually waste twenty minutes telling stories until we get into doing the scene, but with her, it's, "We work." Rehearsals go well. There's a young actress, Simone Griffeth, who plays Bea's daughter-in-law, and that's the only bone of contention. Bea hates her, and if Bea doesn't like you, look out. I try to keep them apart. If I'm going to shoot a scene that doesn't have to do with Bea, I make sure Bea has gone to her dressing room before I start rehearsing with Simone. If Bea is on the set watching, she says, "What is she doing? That's not acting. It's stupid."

Unlike the main character in *Fawlty Towers*, Bea is widowed. In one episode, Kevin McCarthy plays her late husband's brother, a white hunter who's so out of touch, he doesn't even know his brother has died. He stays at the inn and he winds up in a little romance with Bea. On the big night, she goes up to Kevin's room. He's got a bottle of champagne and music playing. He's a guy that's been around, while she has never been with anybody but her husband. Bea and I talk about how her character feels like a sixteen-year-old virgin who's going to make love for the first time. We get into the bedroom and an idea pops into my head. I tell Bea, "I'm gonna give you one note and I think it should carry you through the scene: The bed is your enemy." Bea gets it immediately and she's simply hilarious in the scene. She walks towards the bed, looks at it, then walks away. She's talking to Kevin and she sits down on the bed by accident, then jumps up. That sort of thing. We do a run-through for producer Allan Manings, who says, "Bea, that business with the bed is wonderful." She tells him, "Howard. All Howard." I've never had an actor say that before. When Allan Manings is brought in to replace the original producers the second week I do the show, Bea tells Allan, "Howard directs *all* of them."

My old acting teacher, Jeff Corey, is set to guest-star on another episode. I tell Allan, "I don't want to knock the guy out of a job, but I'm uncomfortable, because he was my acting teacher and I feel funny directing him." Allan says, "It'll be fine." Jeff comes in and I tell him, "I feel a little weird directing you." He tells me, "Howard, direct me like you would direct any actor. Forget that I taught. Now I'm an actor and I'm depending on you for direction." It turns out to be an absolute joy working with Jeff. Of all the shows I've done, Allan Manings is the only one to send me a letter thanking me for my professionalism, for getting everything I could out of what they gave me, and always being out on time. It's a very sweet letter and it's a pleasure working with him.

In the spring of 1983, I get a call from Woody Allen's office telling me, "Mr. Allen would like you to be in his new film." I ask, "What's the name of it?" They tell me, "I'm sorry, but we're not at liberty to say." I ask, "Can you send me some pages?" They tell me, "I'm sorry, but Mr. Allen doesn't send out scripts. Do you want to do it?" I say, "Yeah." I get on the plane and I'm sitting next to Sandy Baron. Sandy's going to impress me. He says, "I'm flying to New York to do Woody Allen's new movie." I tell him, "That's interesting. So am I." The film will eventually be called *Broadway Danny Rose*.

We get to New York and we're put up at the Essex House on Central Park South. Around the corner is the Park Central Hotel on 7th Avenue, where Jackie Gleason used to live. It's about a block up from the Carnegie Deli. That's where they set up a suite of dressing rooms for the comics. I have no idea why the dressing rooms aren't at the Essex House. We have a nine o'clock call, so they send limos to pick us up at the Essex House just to take us around the corner to the Park Central! Every comic in New York knows we're there doing Woody's movie, so everybody we know drops in to the suite to schmooze and nosh. It's great seeing some of my old Manhattan pals again after living in L.A. for a dozen years. They send up platters of lox and smoked whitefish and bagels and cream cheese. We sit there and talk and laugh and tell stories. We're having a ball. Jack Rollins, Woody's producer and the man who, along with Charlie Joffe, changed my life, is taking it all in.

About three o'clock, they call us to come down to the Carnegie Deli to shoot our scenes. We're already "prepped" from eating deli food and swapping stories and laughing in the hotel. It gives us sort of a running start into doing the scenes. We take our seats at the table and then I ask Woody, "Do you want us to stay with the script?" Woody says, "No, just make sure you say certain things, like the setup about how there are no nightclubs anymore. And I need you to mention the hypnotist in the Catskills who hypnotized a woman who couldn't come out of it." We ad-lib most of it, making sure to hit the important lines, but we basically just continue what we've been doing at the Park Central Hotel before leaving for the deli. At one point, Woody comes by our table, because he wants to give us direction. We're talking away and he's standing there, not wanting to interrupt us. Finally, he finds a space and he says, "Listen..." We say, "Woody, please, we're busy here." He loves it and it's a lot of fun for all of us. The fellow who plays the waiter in that scene is an actual waiter at the Carnegie Deli. When we break for lunch, we move to another table and continue eating our corned-beef sandwiches – and the waiter who waits on us is the same guy who's *playing* the waiter who waits on us in the movie! That really strikes me as funny. We enjoy that huge, delicious spread at the Park Central Hotel, then we're eating in the scenes at the Carnegie Deli – and then we break for lunch! All that food! It's like being on a cruise, without the ocean. By breaking for lunch at the Carnegie, Woody is able to keep us all corralled, because with comics, you let one guy wander off on his own and pretty soon, everybody scatters to different places.

We shoot the deli scenes in about two or three days and then, as we're leaving, I tell Woody, "Thanks. It was great seeing you." He says, "I'll probably see you again in July." I ask, "Oh, are you coming out to California?" He says, "No, I'll probably want to reshoot the scene." That's what he does. He gets what he's got, he edits together an assemblage of footage, he looks at the scene and then he thinks, "I can do a better joke here. I can add a joke there." He's the only director I know of that has that power, and the reason is because he takes a lot less money, but he gets control of his films. Also, since he likes to shoot at real locations instead of building sets, he knows the Carnegie Deli will still be there if he needs to reshoot the scene. As promised, Sandy Baron and I go back to New York in July for a day of reshoots. Woody tells us the things he needs us to do and explains how they'll fit into the existing footage. Diane Sawyer is there, too, although I'm not sure why. Before we start shooting, she's at the head of the table and Sandy is hitting on her. I keep thinking to myself, "Is he kidding? Does he really think he has a shot with her?" She isn't married to Mike Nichols yet, but still! Woody gets what he needs from us and cuts those into the film. *Broadway Danny Rose* turns out to be a pretty terrific picture.

CHAPTER TWENTY-EIGHT

After *Mork & Mindy* runs its course, one of the show's writers, Ed Scharlach, teams up with Sam Goldwyn Jr.'s wife, Peggy, to write scripts. One day, Sam asks Ed, "Do you know of a television director that can work fast and knows comedy?" Ed says, "Yeah, Howard Storm." Another writer, Wally Dalton, has a meeting with Sam about another project and he's asked the same question. Wally answers, "Yeah, Howard Storm." I get a call from Mr. Goldwyn, who tells me, "It's really interesting. I spoke to two different people and both of them gave me your name." Sam gives me a script called *Once Bitten*. I read it, then meet with him to discuss it. We agree on the script's strengths and weaknesses, then make a deal to do the movie. It's a terrific experience.

The film isn't intended as a Jim Carrey vehicle. We see a load of different actors, but when Jim comes in, he really connects. We read him two or three times before we sign him. Jim is very easy to work with and he's very happy to have the lead in a movie, because this is his first feature film. The writers and producers want to go with Cassandra Petersen – TV's Elvira, Mistress of the Dark – for the female vampire lead. I tell them, "That's a cartoon. That's ridiculous. I don't want to do that. Let's get a real actress to play it," so we bring in Lauren Hutton, who is just wonderful in the part.

As originally written, Lauren's assistant is a bald, heavyset mute. He doesn't say a word in the entire film. I say, "To make it more interesting, why don't we get a black guy who's very elegant and erudite and proper?" The first one we go after is Roscoe Lee Browne. I did a bit with him in a TV movie called *The Big Rip-Off* ten years earlier and I think he's terrific. Roscoe isn't available, so we go with Cleavon Little, who's so great in *Blazing Saddles*. He's a pleasure to work with, a great actor, and he knows where "funny" is. Changing Lauren's assistant from a heavyset mute white guy to Cleavon Little brings a whole new tone to the film.

In the script, Jim Carrey's two friends work in a hamburger joint. I say, "Jim should have a job, too. If his two friends work, it looks a little strange if he's not working. But we need to find a job where he can be out and about, because he has to run into Lauren." We come up with an ice cream truck that he drives after school and that works out nicely.

Sam Goldwyn Jr. screens *Terminator* for me and suggests Polish cinematographer, Adam Greenberg, as my Director of Photography. I tell him, "His stuff looks great." We set up a lunch meeting with Adam and the producer and throughout the entire meeting, all I get from Adam is "Yes" and "No." I can't get any conversation going with him. Later, I tell Sam, "I have to be able to communicate with my cinematographer, but I got nothing from him except yeses and nos. I've got to have a guy that relates to me." Sam says, "Would you be willing to fly to Vegas where Adam's shooting a movie and discuss that with him and maybe give him a second shot?" I tell him, "Sure." I go to Vegas and Adam takes me to a Chinese restaurant, then proceeds to tell me his amazing life story about being a little boy in Poland when the Nazis invaded, escaping with his family to Israel, and eventually becoming a cameraman. After that, we get along great and I'm delighted to bring him onboard as our cinematographer.

As a first-time feature-film director, I'm a little shaky, so Adam helps me a lot. I set up one shot and he tells me, "Y'know, Howard, I was thinking: Why don't we put the camera here and then move the camera? Then we wind up where you wanted to start your shot." I say, "In other words, you're saying, 'Move the camera. Don't be static.'" I'm so used to working on weekly television shows, I don't always think of creative ways to use the camera.

We're shooting the scene where Lauren seduces Jim. I decide to shoot it in sequence. The last shot of the night is Lauren telling Jim, "I'm going to go upstairs and slip into something more comfortable." In the morning, we're going to shoot her coming down the steps in a negligee, looking very sexy. I add a moment where she bites the buttons off of his shirt, top to bottom, one at a time, and spits them out, then her head disappears out of frame. It's a lot of sexy fun. The next morning, I come to the set and I have all my shots set up. I talk things over with Adam and we're ready to go. Suddenly, Lauren appears at the top of the stairs wearing black lipstick and black nail polish and her hair is in a completely different style than it was the previous night. I ask Lauren, "What is this? You go up to change into a negligee and you take all of your makeup off and you put fresh makeup on, take all your nail polish off and put fresh nail polish on and you change your hair-do? That would take two and a half hours." She says, "I want to look sexy for him." I tell her, "That's ridiculous. No woman in the world that wants to seduce a guy would go upstairs and take two and a half hours to get ready." I turn to the makeup guy and ask, "Who allowed this?" He says, "She told me you said it was okay." I call the heads of all the departments together and I tell them, "Nobody accepts anything unless you come to me and clear it first." I lose two and a half hours. Lauren has to go back, take off all the makeup, and get back to looking like she did when she went upstairs. All through the shoot, Lauren is telling me, "I should have spiked hair." I tell her, "Your character wouldn't have spiked hair." She says, "Oh, but it would look so cool!" I tell her, "Lauren, when you direct your own movie, you can have spiked hair, but I'm directing this one." She calls me a wuss, but she has a great personality and I really love working with her. In another scene, Lauren is in the dressing room of a department store and Ted, the lighting director, is up on a ladder, setting the light. Lauren calls out, "Ted!" He looks down just as she flashes her tits at him. He almost falls off the ladder. She does goofy things like that constantly, which is a lot of fun.

I find a spot to put my kids, Casey and Anthony, in the film. They ride their bikes up to Jim Carrey to buy ice cream. Jim turns around and he's got the vampire fangs and they both take off running. I have the camera set up so that when Jim turns around and looks in the mirror, he sees the steeple of a church behind him and he runs into the church to talk to a priest. I tell Adam, "When he comes into the church, I'd like to put a camera up in the balcony and shoot down on him with a wide lens. As he walks down the aisle, we tilt up and reveal the entire church." Getting that shot requires a lot of lighting and a lot of hiding of the lights.

Adam says, "You know what we can do? I can lay some track and we can follow him and see the archways and then we'll get to the altar." I tell him, "I want it to be Chaplinesque. I want it to look like he's in this giant church and he's a small figure who's all alone, so I want the wide lens and I want it up high so that he looks smaller than he really is. Then we tilt up and reveal the whole church." Adam is trying to avoid the problems and the time it will take to light a scene like that. The producer comes in and says, "Adam's right. You can just lay some track." I tell him, "I know, but I want that shot. I know it's going to take a long time to set up the lights, but I'm willing to take some other shots out to make up for it, because this is important to me." We do it my way and at the dailies, Sam turns to me and says, "Howard, that is a *great* shot!"

In another scene, Cleavon disappears into the kitchen. You can't see him, but you hear glasses tinkling and then he appears with a tray and he goes up a staircase. He makes a turn and continues going up the steps. I want the camera to follow him up, which means putting a high hat on the camera, which is a metal attachment that gives you more space to shoot. Poor Adam has to stand on his *toes* in order to look into the frame, but we get the shot and it works out fine. Then I notice that at the top of the set, there's a ledge that isn't painted, because it wasn't going to be in the shot as originally planned. Every time I watch the movie, I notice that, but I don't think anybody else does.

I'm as stubborn about the material as I am about getting the shots I want. In the original version of the scene where Jim goes into the church, there's a homeless wino, played by Gary Goodrow from The Committee. He's sitting in a confessional and he turns to the priest through the little window, asking, "Do you have any toilet paper? I'm all out." I tell the writers, "There's no way I'm going to shoot this joke." I tell Sam, "I'm not shooting this joke. The guy is *shitting* in a confessional in a church! It's insulting to Catholics and it's insulting to me – and I'm not a Catholic." We're having lunch and one of the producers, Robby Wald, comes into the restaurant. He gets on his knees and says, "Please, please! You gotta do that joke! Without that joke, the movie *dies!*" I tell him, "Robby, what the hell are you talking about? It's not gonna die. It's one joke and not even a good joke. It's a tasteless joke and I'm not gonna shoot it. That's it." I stand my ground, we change the gag to something else, and it's fine.

Years later, I'm having lunch with Sam Goldwyn Jr. and I tell him, "Y'know, I think I made a mistake by sitting on Jim Carrey and holding him down, because I didn't want him to be too over-the-top." Sam says, "I think you're right. I should've seen that, too." But while we're shooting, I don't want him mugging. I want him to be real, because he's a teenager who's being followed by a beautiful woman that he doesn't realize is a vampire. If I'd really let Jim run with it, it would've been a different movie. It would've been a cartoon. Nevertheless, I am very proud of *Once Bitten* and it remains a high point of my career.

CHAPTER TWENTY-NINE

My next project isn't a feature film, but it *is* a classy production and a wonderful experience: *Fairie Tale Theater* for Shelley Duvall. It's an adaptation of *The Three Little Pigs*, starring Billy Crystal, Stephen Furst, Fred Willard and Jeff Goldblum. Furst is, appropriately, the "first" pig that builds a house out of straw. Fred Willard plays the pig that builds a wooden house. Billy is the third pig that builds a house out of bricks. Jeff Goldbum plays the wolf. I give him a note: "Think Harlem pimp." Jeff is six-three, six-four to begin with, but we have him in lifts and with the big hat, he looks like he's nine feet tall! He comes to the set and he says, "Hey, little piggies! What's happenin'?" When he says, "I'll huff and I'll puff and I'll blow your house down!" we have a vest rigged with an air hose running up his leg to inflate his chest and puff it way out.

Larry Hankin, my old pal from The Committee, plays the huckster who sells them their building materials. I tell him, "You know Sid Stone, the guy on Milton Berle who would say, 'Tell ya what I'm gonna do'? That's how you should play this guy. 'Tell ya what I'm gonna do. You look to me like a straw guy. Y'know, straw is the perfect building material. It can be *very* strong.' That kind of thing." At first, Larry says, "Eh, I don't know," but I tell him, "Larry, at least *try* it." When he sees it, Larry tells me, "You were so right."

The music is fun, too, because they have a different instrument representing each of the different pigs, like in *Peter and the Wolf*. When we go into the studio to record the music, I get an extra kick because the tenor sax player is Bob Cooper, who had been with Stan Kenton's band and who had married Kenton's vocalist, June Christy. I tell Bob that when Lou Alexander and I were partners, we opened for June in Daytona Beach when we were nineteen years old.

It's a classy show and a great experience. Shelley Duvall asks me back to do that episode of *Tall Tales & Legends* with Steve

Guttenberg as Pecos Bill and Rebecca De Mornay as Martin Mull's daughter, Slew Foot Sue. Everyone is a pleasure to work with and it's another fun show to do.

After my acting stint in *Broadway Danny Rose*, I wind up in another film, *The Check is in the Mail*, directed by Ted Kotcheff, who brings me in to play Anne Archer's psychiatrist. Anne comes to see me in my office and I'm eating jellybeans during our session. Suddenly, I have a heart attack and die. She panics, afraid she'll be implicated in my death, so she looks through my appointment book and tears out the page with her name on it. It's a fun little bit that allows me to exercise my acting chops.

In 1986, I'm brought in to direct several episodes of *The Redd Foxx Show*, in which Redd owns a luncheonette and lives with an adopted white teenage girl. One day, I give a note to my Production Assistant and tell her to take it to Redd. She goes into his trailer and he's standing there completely naked. He grabs her, so she runs out of the trailer. The second time this happens, she comes to me and says, "You know, I need this job, I'm raising a kid on my own, I need the money, but I can't do this," and she quits. Sadly, she doesn't feel she can press charges without being blacklisted as a troublemaker. This was decades before the #MeToo movement changed all that.

For Redd, everything is filtered through the racial prism. Redd's neighbor is a semi-recurring character who owns a furniture store next to the luncheonette. He complains to Redd that he's paying for TV ads featuring Ricky the Raccoon and they aren't drumming up business. We have a read-through on the first day and Redd says, "You can't say 'raccoon.'" I ask him, "Why not? It's just an animal." Redd tells me, "You don't get it, man. 'Raccoon' sounds too much like 'coon.' It sounds like you're callin' somebody a coon." I say, "Look, Redd, it's silly to worry about this. Let's change it to Sammy the Squirrel and then we don't have a problem, okay?" Well, it's *not* okay. Redd won't let it go. He continues: "Lemme explain somethin' to you, baby. You're directing this. They see your name and you happen to be in Harlem and they know you're the guy that directed the thing where somebody said 'raccoon,' they'll stick a damn *knife* in you, man! I'm tryin' to *help* you! Don't you get it?"

No sooner do we clear that hurdle than another one crops up. There's a scene where Redd is sick and goes to the doctor, who tells his adopted daughter she'll have to make special foods for him. Back home in the kitchen, she puts down a bowl of what are supposed to be mashed lima beans. Redd asks, "What's this?" She says, "Lima beans. They're just mashed up." Whatever the prop guys cook up looks like a bowl of grits. I ask, "Where's the prop guy? They're lima beans. They should look green." Redd says, "Lima beans ain't green. They white." I tell him, "Redd, lima beans are not white; they're a light green." Redd says, "Lemme tell ya somethin', man. Ain't no nigger in the world gonna eat no green lima beans. They white!" He calls over to a guy named Major, one of his buddies on the show: "You ever hear of anybody eatin' green lima beans? Ain't they *always* white?" Major says, "Yeah." Redd says, "See? I *told* ya!" I tell him, "At this point, I don't give a shit whether they're green or white. Let's just move on."

There's a scene where Redd's daughter doesn't want to go to college. She tells Redd, "You didn't go to college and you did okay." His reply, as written, is, "Yeah, but if I went to college, I coulda become president. My face would look *good* on a dollar." Redd changes the line to, "My face would look *good* on all that money." I tell him, "Redd, adding those words throws it off. Just say, 'My face would look good on a dollar.'" He says, "No, man, you don't understand it. Comedy is exaggeration, so I'm sayin' 'all that money'!" We go back and forth on this, just as we go back and forth on everything else. I get a call from the producers: "Can you come up to the office? We'd like to talk to you." I walk in and they say, "Redd says you don't respect him." I tell them, "That's the first time he's been right all week." But I get it: They have a star and they need to protect him. I finish up the last of my three shows and then I'm gone.

Next up is *Perfect Strangers* with Mark-Linn Baker and Bronson Pinchot. The show is basically *Laverne & Shirley* in drag, and nowhere is that more evident than in the show I am to direct. Ten years earlier, I direct an episode of *Laverne & Shirley* called, "Drive, She Said" where Laverne is learning how to drive. My episode of *Perfect Strangers* is called "Baby You Can Drive My Car," where Balki is learning how to drive. For all intents and purposes, I already directed this show ten years earlier. On *Laverne & Shirley*, Cindy teaches Penny how to drive using a grapefruit and a banana to represent the brake and the accelerator. The dialogue is: "Okay, now step on the banana. No! You're going too fast! Step on the grapefruit! The grapefruit!" It's funny and it works. We do the same thing for Larry and Balki, using a watermelon and a cantaloupe as the pedals. There may be different writers credited on those two shows, but they are the same show – only the fruit has been changed to protect the innocent.

When Sammy Shore divorces his wife Mitzi, The Comedy Store falls under Mitzi's ownership. Mitzi builds it up into what it has become, but she's very difficult. She's charging a five-dollar cover to see the show, but refusing to give the performers a cent, saying she's doing them a big favor by giving them a showcase. This is a woman who was married to a comic, so she should understand how important it is for them to get paid, but Mitzi doesn't budge. She doesn't even give them cab fare to get to and from The Comedy Store. Her hard line leads to a strike in 1979, when the comedians refuse to perform until Mitzi starts paying them, which she does – *very* reluctantly.

In 1986, Mitzi asks me to direct a special for Showtime called *Girls of the Comedy Store*, featuring Shirley Hemphill and Carrie Snow, amongst other female comedians. It's a combination of standup and sketches. I tell Mitzi, "If I agree to direct it, you cannot be around, telling me to do this and do that. You've gotta back off." I know her and I know her reputation for being domineering. She agrees and it actually goes very smoothly. Every so often, she suggests something like, "Wouldn't it be funnier if we heard a toilet flush?" and I tell her, "No, actually it wouldn't," and that's the end of it.

But Seriously Folks is sort of a recreation of the Carnegie Deli roundtable in *Broadway Danny Rose*, with a bunch of comedians telling funny stories about their experiences in show business. Bob Weide is the producer and I'm directing it. We get Shecky Greene, Corbett Monica and Jan Murray, with Garry Marshall as the emcee. It's a great setup and great fun. I suggest we do it like they're sitting around someone's living room or den, noshing on cream cheese and lox and bagels and so on. Jan Murray tells some Henny Youngman stories that are just hilarious. Corbett says, "This comic I knew was in a hotel room with a woman and he had her tied up. All of a sudden, there's loud banging on the door. A guy yells, 'Fire!' and the comic yells, 'What floor?'"

Our only real problem is how to cut down the lengthy stories and not lose which celebrity they're talking about. At one point, everybody's talking about Frank Sinatra, but when we edit that sequence, we realize we've edited out Frank's name in the middle of a lengthy chunk. I find a spot where Corbett puts his hand in front of his mouth and clears his throat and I say, "That's it! Wipe the cough and put 'Sinatra' in there." It works! Bob Weide and I get the show down to a half-hour. We're pleased with it and so are the comics. It's done as a pilot with the idea of rotating different comics each week, but to our disappointment, it's not picked up. I'm shocked, because the reaction to the show is so terrific.

I don't know what Scoey Mitchell had on Brandon Tartikoff, but Brandon buys a pilot from him – twice. In 1986, Scoey brings me in for what turns out to be seven episodes of one of them – *Mr. & Mrs. C.* Neither one of us mentions the lawsuit over *B.C. & Me* some years earlier. Scoey does not like to spend money on a show, even though Brandon gives him $350,000 to shoot each episode. Scoey refuses to rent typewriters for the writers, so they have to write on legal pads! At one point, another production company comes in and the staff has to move upstairs to the second floor. Scoey won't hire movers, so the writers have to carry all their files and desks and office furniture upstairs themselves. The craft services table is a joke. It's like chewing gum and cookies.

I have to reshoot the pilot that Scoey shot. There's a scene where Mrs. C, played by Peg Murray, and her daughter, played by Ellen Regan, go to a bank. The way the set is built, you can't get a good angle on the two women. I tell the prop man, "Put a hole in the wall and we'll put the camera there. That way, we get a nice two-shot." Scoey comes down to the set, sees the hole in the wall and goes nuts: "Who did this?!" I tell him, "I did." He says, "Are you crazy?! You put a hole in the wall! I *own* that set!" I tell him, "I know you own it. That's why I put the hole in the wall. If the set was rented, I wouldn't have done it. I'm trying to get decent shots for you and I needed to do that. Just put a picture over the hole after we shoot." Scoey says, "What if I don't *want* to put a picture over it?" I tell him, "Then you've got a hole in your wall." Everybody breaks up and he settles down.

The control booth has a door with a little glass window and a sliding bolt so you can lock it. Whenever something goes wrong, Scoey runs up and opens the door, screaming, "Why'd you miss that shot?!" or whatever the problem is. One day, I miss a shot and I know he's on his way, so I walk over and I slide the bolt closed, locking him out. He has no idea it's locked, so he almost tears his arm off grabbing the handle and yanking it as hard as he can. Everybody in the booth is hysterical. He's looking through the window and I see fire in his eyes. He finally realizes how ridiculous he looks, so he smiles and then I go over and open the door.

On one show, he hires a guy to play a preacher and he just isn't cutting it. We do the run-through and Scoey tells me, "We've got to replace him." I say, "Scoey, you know what would be great? If *you* played it." He says, "No, I can't do that." I want him to play the part so he'll be so busy working on his lines, he won't be bothering me and driving everybody nuts. Eventually, I talk him into playing the preacher and of the seven episodes that I direct, it's the easiest one. Scoey and I actually get along a lot more often than not. Years earlier, when he's doing the black version of *Barefoot in the Park* for ABC, Scoey gets into an argument with Executive Producer Doug Cramer, punching him in the face and breaking his nose. All things considered, I got off pretty easily in terms of Scoey's anger management.

In 1988, I direct two episodes of *Just the Ten of Us*, starring my old pal, the scene-setting pantomime artist from *Where Has Tommy Flowers Gone?*, Bill Kirchenbauer. It's great working with Bill, seeing him succeed and having his own series. In one episode, we have a boxing scene between two twelve-year-old boys. I call one of my contacts in the boxing world and tell him I need two amateurs around twelve years old. One of them is an absolutely adorable kid named Shane Mosley. When he starts fighting professionally, I tell sportswriter and commentator Larry Merchant, "This kid has really got something." Shane's father talks to Larry about bringing Shane to HBO. Shane Mosley goes on to become the Lightweight Champion of the World, beating Oscar De La Hoya – twice – among other notable prizefighters. It's nice to see I still have an eye for spotting potential champs.

CHAPTER THIRTY

In 1986, Executive Producers Bob Boyett and Tom Miller bring me in to direct *Valerie*, a new series starring my old *Rhoda* compatriot, Valerie Harper. When I started working with Val on *Rhoda*, I didn't really know what I was doing, but in the intervening years, I've become a much more skilled director. By the time Val and I are working on a series again, I'm an old hand. I come in around the middle of the season and do two shows. I worked for Tom Miller before, Val is always great to work with, and I like the co-star, Jason Bateman, so working on *Valerie* is really a very pleasant experience.

At first.

Valerie is becoming increasingly unhappy because the focus of the show is shifting away from her and toward Jason. Girls are falling in love with him and rightfully so; he's a good-looking, talented kid. The season ends and when it's time to return, Valerie tells the Executive Producers, "I love Jason. He's a wonderful actor and a lovely guy, but this is not the show I signed on for. This is supposed to be about a woman raising three boys. I'm not coming back unless you do the show we agreed on originally." They tell her everything will work out just fine. In the meantime, we do one episode with scenes missing for Valerie to do after everything gets straightened out and she returns. She comes back to the set and there's a huge banner, "WELCOME HOME, VALERIE!" with a big cake and a party. She asks me, "How many shows are you doing this season?" I tell her, "I don't know yet. They haven't made a deal with me." She says, "I'm meeting with them on Monday and I want you to do *all* of them, the whole season." I tell her, "Fine with me!"

Then Valerie gets the first two scripts and she sees that instead of focusing more on her character, they've actually *added* two young guys to be Jason's buddies, and most of the story takes place at his high school. Valerie meets with the producers and they have a horrendous fight, after which, they *fire* her, even though they have no legitimate grounds – and NBC allows it to happen. Rumors start going around that Valerie has been fired because she's asking for too much money, but it's never about the money. They've had it with her complaining and they keep lying to try to placate her. The entire time, they have Sandy Duncan in the background, in case they need a new star. I get a call from Valerie saying, "You won't believe it. They fired me!" I ask her, "How can they *fire* you?" She says, "I don't know, but they did. My lawyer says I should send them a telegram asking what time they want me in for wardrobe on Tuesday, to show them I'm ready to work." She does so and they ignore it. Valerie rightfully sues NBC and Miller-Boyett for wrongful termination.

NBC's argument is that Valerie is disruptive and costs the company money. I'm called in to give a deposition. The lawyer from NBC asks me, "Isn't it true that you were directing a scene in the kitchen between Miss Harper and Mr. Bateman and Miss Harper was so angry in the scene that you had to shoot it two times after the audience left?" I reply, "Yes, but that's not unusual. Many times, we shoot a scene after the audience has left. In this case, there was very little comedy in the scene, so it made sense to shoot it after the audience had left. Also, as a director, I gave her the note to play it angry, because I thought the situation called for it." "The situation" is that a new girl comes to town and Jason dates her. His friends ask him what happened and he coyly remains silent, letting them draw their own conclusions, so they figure he must've scored. As a result, all the girls in school call her a slut and all the guys are hitting on her. I tell Valerie, "Your character would be very angry that her son caused this. It's so anti-woman and so mean-spirited, you should really bang him around." I tell the NBC attorney, "Yes, we did shoot the scene two times after the audience left. The first time, the producers thought she was not angry enough; the second time, they said, 'Fine.'" Eventually, I finish my deposition.

Instead of settling, the case goes to jury trial and I'm called to the stand. Why the NBC attorney asks me the same questions, I don't know. I'm thinking to myself, "Is he trapping me? What's going on? I told him answers he didn't want to hear during the deposition, so why is he asking me the same questions again in front of a jury?" Finally, he asks, "Would it be fair to say that Miss Harper is responsible for your becoming a director?" I reply, "I think that's fair, because my first directing job was on *Rhoda* and if Miss Harper didn't want me to do it, then I wouldn't have gotten it." He asks, "Would it be fair to say that you and Miss Harper are good friends?" I answer, "Yes, that's fair." He says, "So there's nothing you wouldn't do for her." I tell him, "That's not true." He asks, "What wouldn't you do?" and I answer, "Lie." The jury gasps. I see Valerie's lawyer lean over and whisper in her ear. Later, she tells me he whispered, "He just won your case."

They have to pay Valerie $80,000 a week for twenty weeks and they have to pay Tony Cacciotti, Valerie's husband and the producer of the show, $10,000 a week for twenty weeks. Then they give me a contract to direct six episodes at the end of the season, which means I'm out of work until towards the end. I'm offered a job that's going to conflict with one of those six shows, so I go to the guy who's set to direct the next show and I ask him, "I have a job. Can you switch a date with me?" He says, "Sure." Next thing I know, the producers won't allow it. They're *very* angry at me. They're so angry at Valerie that when it comes time to write her out of the series, instead of having her move away or needing to go off somewhere and she might return, they have a fire break out inside the house. She runs back in to get the dog and she dies in the fire. I'm the one who has to shoot that scene. We have fire trucks outside the house and they fake a fire for the cameras. It's a very dramatic scene, with Jason standing in the doorway, looking at a photo of Valerie. We do a rack focus from Valerie's face in the picture to Jason's face as he looks at it. They must've had so much fun writing this, knowing they're killing Valerie off and she's going to die in a fire.

The producers protect themselves by giving me those six episodes, because if they didn't give me *any*, I'd have a lawsuit against them for unfairly cutting me loose. I direct those six shows – and then I'm promptly blacklisted at Lorimar. The president at that time is Leslie Moonves. Lorimar is bought up by Warner Brothers, so I'm also blacklisted at Warner Brothers. Then Leslie becomes president of CBS, so I'm blacklisted at CBS. I don't work for *two and a half years*, because of the blacklist.

In 1992, I get a job at Warner Brothers, of all places. It's a show called *Scorch*, about a miniature dragon. I come in and direct an episode on which Dr. Joyce Brothers is guest starring. They ask me to do another one the following week, and then I get a call from my agent saying, "They went *nuts* over at Warner Brothers. They don't know how you slipped past the radar and they don't want you to do the next show." I tell him, "Okay, let it go." Allan Katz, who is the producer of *Scorch*, calls and asks, "Jesus, what happened? They called me into the office and they reamed my ass! 'How *dare* you book Howard Storm!'" I tell him, "Allan, it's okay. Don't worry about it. They don't want me to do the next one and I'm not going to hold them up for it, so you're clean." I could've said, "I want my money!" because they committed themselves to a second show, but I figure just let it go. One guy at Warner Brothers takes it on as a personal vendetta and will not let me work there, claiming he doesn't like my work. I want to take it to court. My plan is to run a *Taxi* episode that Jim Burrows directed, with no name on it, and one that I directed, with no name on it, and then ask him, "Tell me, which is the terrible show? Who's the bad director?" My lawyer tells me I have no case, so once again, I let it go.

One of my close friends, Frank Pace, who produces at Warner Brothers, wants me to direct *Suddenly Susan*, but they won't allow it. Frank wants me to do *The George Lopez Show*, but they won't allow it. All this because I had the temerity to tell the truth on the stand in the Valerie Harper case. Even with the pain of not getting work for two and a half years, I would do it again. Grips and guys I worked with run into my kids and tell them, "Your father is a special guy. He didn't cop out. He stood up. When everybody else was copping out, he did the right thing." The important thing for me is that my sons understand what it is to be honest and a good friend and to stand up. That, to me, is more important than all of this crap. It's a great lesson to them and they take great pride in it. One of my sons tells me, "I met a guy at the studio and he said, 'You're Howard Storm's son? Your father is some great guy! He didn't back off!'" It's worth going through it all, just to hear that.

In 1990, Valerie Harper calls me and says, "I'm doing another series. I want you to do the pilot and I want you to do all the shows, but you have to meet Paul Haggis, because he created it." We meet with Paul. He agrees and, true to Val's word, I direct all of them. It's called *City* because Val plays the City Manager of an unnamed city – we have Detroit in mind – and it takes place around the mayor's office in City Hall. It has the potential of being a very good show. In the pilot, there's a huge rainstorm that pushes out a lot of mud, and caskets from the cemetery roll into Val's jurisdiction. It's a funny premise, with Val and the cemetery owner arguing about who has to clean it up.

At first, we can't find a comedy editor to cut the show; they're all busy working on other series. We take a young editor who's only done drama. He's a good editor, but he doesn't understand humor. He edits the show and I'm looking at it, along with Val's husband Tony Cacciotti and Paul Haggis. I tell Paul, "You wrote a very funny script, but there's nothing funny here. We've got to go in and edit from frame one." So that's what I do, adding a few frames here and a few frames there, all along the way, tightening it up and leaving room for laughs. We spend two full days reediting the show, but it fixes the comedy timing and Tony tells me I saved Paul's ass.

Working with Paul is not easy. He's an obsessive micromanager. He decides that in a scene in Valerie's office, co-star Stephen Lee is too over-the-top and we need to reshoot the scene. CBS and MTM ask me, "Why are we reshooting the scene?" I tell them, "I don't have a problem with it, but your Exec wants to reshoot it because he thinks Steve is over-the-top." I ask Paul, "You're okay with Valerie, right?" He says, "Yes." I tell him, "Good. I'm gonna sit Valerie next to the camera and she'll do her lines and he can play off of that." Paul and I are looking at a video of the original scene and at one point, Steve leans in and we see a small piece of Valerie. Paul yells, "Valerie's in the shot! Get her in makeup and wardrobe!" I tell him, "Whoa, whoa, wait a minute! She's not in the shot. This was what we shot *before* and now we're reshooting it." Tony is flipping out, because by now it's 1:30 in the morning. He says, "That's it, Val; we're going." Paul tells him, "I'm the Exec Producer. She stays until I say she can leave." Tony says, "Why don't we discuss this in the parking lot?" and he turns and starts to walk away. Paul is walking after him. I grab Paul and I ask, "Do you understand

what he means?" He says, "Sure. He wants to talk about the scene."
I tell him, "Paul, if you go out there, he'll bounce your head off every
fender in the parking lot. Do you think you could beat him in a
fight?" He says, "No." I tell him, "Then don't go out." That's the end
of that. We do thirteen episodes and then CBS declines to pick it
up, which is a shame, because it's a good show with a great cast of
funny people, including Todd Susman and Liz Torres.

During the run of *City*, I take Paul Haggis to Las Vegas, where
he sees his very first prizefight. Fifteen years later, he wins the Best
Original Screenplay Oscar for *Million Dollar Baby*.

Paul Haggis' manager, Mark Harris, becomes partners in an
agency with David Shapira and I sign with them. I get a call from
an agent in the office telling me she got me an episode of *Alf* to
direct. As it turns out, the deal they make only gives me Directors
Guild minimum, so I call David and I tell him, "I haven't worked
for minimum since a year after I started directing." David says,
"Jesus, I'm sorry, but there's nothing I can do, because we agreed to
take it. Tell you what; I won't take a commission on this." I tell him,
"Thanks, but more important than that, I need you to write them
a letter saying that if they want me to do more, they'll pay my fee."
So we write them the letter.

The Exec Producer is Tom Patchett, who was part of a comedy
act that I saw when I was playing Mister Kelly's in Chicago. I do
Alf and I have a great time. Unlike Wayland and Madame, Alf isn't
treated like a sentient creature when the cameras are off. The way
they handle him is actually quite clever. They build the stage up on
a platform and then they have trenches running the length of the
set, so that when you walk into the dining room, Alf is below you.
But I never talk to Alf himself; always to the puppeteers.

Mine is the last show of the season. At the wrap party, Tom
Patchett comes up to me and says, "We're *really* happy with your
work. Will you come back and do some more?" I tell him, "I'd be
happy to." Turns out they want me to do them for minimum, so I
say, "Pass," and that's it. It's the only show I know that refuses to pay
more than DGA minimum to any of its directors.

Between the late '80s and the early '90s, I direct ten episodes
of *Head of the Class*. I get to work with my old Committee friend

Howard Hesseman on the first episode, but he has problems with ABC about what the show should be, so they replace him with Billy Connolly, who has never done television. Billy's very nervous, but I get him through it and he's just terrific. He's so good, in fact, that they decide to do a spinoff called *Billy*, in which he plays a Scottish teacher who moves to America. I don't shoot the pilot, but I get to direct four episodes. Years later, I go backstage to see him at a theatre in L.A. and he tells me, "Ah, ya pulled me through it, ya did! I was frightened to death, I tell ya!"

One night, I run into *Webster* creator Stu Silver at the Improv and I ask him, "What's going on?" He says, "I'm gonna be doing a show called *Good Grief*, about a guy who owns a funeral parlor. Oh, shit! *You* should direct them!" And so I do. I direct ten episodes and it's a lot of laughs. We read loads of people for the lead part, including Kevin Pollack and George Segal. We really want George, but Fox insists he's too old. They have Howie Mandel under contract and they're trying to find something for him to do. Howie is great on *St. Elsewhere* and he's a lovely guy and a lot of fun, but he isn't really right for this part. We still have a good time doing the show. Dick Schaal's daughter, Wendy, is the female lead. Tom Poston is terrific as one of the assistants at the funeral parlor. Stu writes in an offbeat "gofer" character played by Sheldon Feldner, who is from San Francisco and has never done television. One day, Sheldon is standing off by a doorway, watching me shoot, so when the camera comes that way, it catches Sheldon in the shot. I yell, "Sheldon, you fuck! You ruined my shot!" After that, his name officially becomes "Sheldon You Fuck." Everybody calls him that.

In the late '80s, my mother has a heart attack and for about a week, my father refuses to visit her in the hospital. When he finally goes to see her, he can only stand in the doorway, looking at her with all the tubes and monitors and so on. Here's this woman that he's loved for so many years, lying there thin and helpless. I get the strong sense that he's really staring at his own mortality. After a while, he turns to me and says, "When I was a young man, I could take a guy out with one punch." It's his way of saying, "I'm falling apart, too." I tell him, "Y'know, Dad, I spoke to Larry Holmes' manager and they don't want to fight you, so I suggest you retire undefeated."

When my father's ninety and my mother's eighty-six, she calls me and says, "Howard, I don't know what to do with him. He's like an *animal.* He wants to make love every night. I can't do it. I'm exhausted. But if I tell him no, he doesn't talk to me all day." I tell her, "Mom, he was the protector of the family, he was a tough guy and now he can hardly walk. Probably the only thing he has left of his manhood is the sex. Maybe there's something you can do for him that'll make him comfortable." She says, "I'm afraid he'll think I'm a *whore.*" Two days later, I get a phone call. She says, "Howard, you should be a doctor. I did what you told me and he's been wonderful." I tell her, "Mom, don't tell me what you did." Not long after, my father Jack Sobel, nee Zeyde Sloboda, passes away at the age of ninety-one.

In the early '90s, a kid who lives across the hall from my mother is playing his music very loud. His place is right off her bedroom and she can't sleep, so she calls and tells me the loud music is keeping her up all night. I say, "Did you ask him to lower the volume?" She says, "A couple of times, but he ignores me." I tell her, "Okay, Mom, I'll come by and see what's goin' on." I go over to her place and we sit down on the couch. Soon enough, we hear a boom box living up to its name – Boom! Boom! Boom! I tell her, "Lemme go talk to him." I ring his bell, but the boom box is so loud, he can't hear me. I start pounding on the door. Finally, the music goes off and I hear, "What is it?" I tell him, "Listen, my mother lives right across the hall from you. She's 88 years old, she's not well, she's asked you a couple of times to lower the music and you ignore her. I want you to listen very carefully, because I'm gonna tell you just once: Lower the volume or you're gonna have yourself a problem. Do you understand what I'm saying?" He says, "Yes." I tell him, "Good. So we're clear now. There won't be any loud music again, right?" He says, "Right." I go back and tell my mother I took care of it. It's peaceful and quiet – for twenty minutes. All of a sudden Boom! Boom! Boom! I tell my mother, "I'm gonna *kill* this guy." I get up and I run at his door. I'm kicking at it, trying to bash the door in. As I'm doing this, I can sense a shadow behind me. I spin around: It's my mother, who's five feet tall and weighs about eighty pounds – with a safe under her arm! I ask her, "Mom, what are you *doing* here?" She says, "There may be *two* of them."

CHAPTER THIRTY-ONE

In 1993, I direct five episodes of *Daddy Dearest* and it's a hilariously funny experience. Richard Lewis is the creator of the series and the star, playing a therapist. Don Rickles is his used-car salesman father and Renee Taylor is his mother. We start rehearsals and Don is getting *screams*. Richard stands there, helpless, saying, "I'm Bud Abbott...I'm Bud Abbott..." Don has no problem saying his lines – as long as the camera isn't rolling. But when the camera rolls, he forgets his lines. One night, we're shooting a show about a school bully picking on Richard's son, played by Jeff Bomberger. Don is going to tell him how to fight and what to do. He says, "'A' is for Adam's Apple. When you hit him there, he'll choke." Whenever Don goes up on his lines, he goes, "unh." So he says, "'A' is for unh." I'm up in the booth. I say, "Don, you want to look at the lines?" Rickles says, "No, I got it. We're okay." We start shooting and Don says, "'A' is for unh." We try it again. This time, Don says, "'A' is for Apple Pan Dowdy." I push the intercom button and say, "Apple Pan Dowdy??" Rickles says, "Why, you have a *better* dessert?"

Don always wears a jogging suit with a zip-up jacket and drawstring pants. During a break in shooting a Halloween show, he stretches the front of his pants way out and says, "Richard! Come say hello to Eddie. I dressed him up for Halloween!" Richard doesn't want anything to do with peering into Don's pants. The cast and crew are standing around watching this and Rickles figures he's got to get *somebody*. "Howie! Come say hello to Eddie. I dressed him up for Halloween!" I walk over, he pulls the front of his pants out, I look down and I say, "Don, how'd you find such a small hat?" Everybody starts to laugh, but that's the end of me, as far as Rickles is concerned. From that point on, he calls me "The Jew Dwarf Director."

Don drives Richard crazy, because Richard is the Executive Producer. If Richard comes to the set ten minutes late, Don announces,

"Well, you have to understand, the man's an *Executive Producer!* He's busy *rewriting!* He's up there *making changes! Fixing the show!* How can he be here on time?" Richard tries to be cool. He doesn't admit it, but he's not happy being teased like that. It's Richard's idea to have Don as his co-star, but I don't think he realizes what that's going to mean on a weekly basis. The pressure of not only being the star but also the Executive Producer of the series is over-whelming for him.

We get a lot of interesting and fun guest stars for the show, includ-ing Huntz Hall – my co-star from *The Manchu Eagle Murder Caper Mystery* – Garrett Morris, Howard Morris, Alice Ghostly, Kaye Ballard and Alex Rocco. One guest star is *particularly* memorable. Don asks if we'd like Frank Sinatra to do the show, adding, "I think I can get him to do it." Of course, we all say yes. Don announces, "Sinatra will be here on Monday, September 13th." Well, we're on hiatus from the beginning of August, but we say okay. Obviously, we're willing to come back and shoot a scene with Frank Sina-tra. All we need is Don, Richard and a few crew members. Frank Pace has saved part of the set, which we're able to dress with slot machines, so you know you're in Vegas. In the show, Rickles is at the casino bar and he starts flirting with a woman, played by Adri-enne Barbeau. It turns out she's the girlfriend of the mobbed-up casino owner, played by Alex Rocco – Moe Greene in *The Godfa-ther*. They send a couple of guys up to Don's room to break his legs, but Richard talks them out of it. He and Don promise to leave the casino and never come back. On their way out of the casino, Don says, "Wow! Look at that dame! She's gorgeous!" Richard says, "Pop, please! Don't start again!" Don says, "What? I only said she's gor-geous!" Then Sinatra is supposed to step into frame and say, "Hey, bullet-head! That's my wife!" Then he walks out of frame. Don and Richard look at each other and think, "Was that...? Nah. Couldn't be." That's the entire scene as written.

We're told Sinatra will be there at twelve o'clock. I know Sinatra will only do one take, so I tell the crew and Richard and Don, "I'm taking no chances. I want you guys in suits and makeup when we get there at ten." Twelve o'clock comes and we get a call from Tony O, Sinatra's guy after Jilly Rizzo dies. He tells us, "Frank just woke up." One o'clock: "Frank's in the shower." Two o'clock: "Frank's having something to eat." Three o'clock: "He's in the car. We're on our way." I tell everybody, "The gate is gonna call me as soon as Mr. Sinatra comes onto the lot. When he comes through the door, we roll cameras and we keep rolling until he leaves the stage. I'm not gonna yell 'Cut.' Cover him wherever he goes."

About three-thirty, the gate calls: "Mr. Sinatra's car just came through." I say, "Okay, everybody! Roll cameras!" I'm standing next to Don. The door opens and in walks Frank Sinatra. He's dramatically backlit, because the sun is behind him at the stage door. He calls out, "Rickles! Where's Rickles?" Frank walks over to where Don and I are standing and Don says, "Go on, Howard. Tell Frank to his *face* what you said about him before!" That's my introduction to Sinatra. Sinatra laughs and says, "Don't pay any attention to him; he's a wiseguy." Frank's wearing a tan windbreaker. He notices that Don and Richard are wearing sport jackets and ties, so he tells Don, "I shoulda worn a jacket!" Rickles says, "Frank, it's not *about* you. Nobody cares." I say, "Mr. Sinatra, I'm Howard Storm. I'm directing the show." He says, "Okay, you wanna run one?" I say, "Sure" and I tell him what I need: "Don and Richard are walking out and Don says, 'What? I only said she was gorgeous.' Then you step into frame and say, 'Hey, bullet-head! That's my wife!' Then you just walk out of frame."

We run through it and Sinatra stays put instead of walking out of frame. He asks, "That okay?" I tell him, "Yeah, I just need you, once you tell him, to turn around and walk out of frame." He says, "Okay, you got it." We do the scene and Sinatra says "Hey, meat-head" instead of "Hey, bullet-head." I don't care. What difference does it make what he calls him? The script supervisor tells me, "He didn't say 'bullet-head.' He said 'meathead.'" I tell him, "I know." He says, "But the script *says* 'bullet-head.' He didn't say it right." I say, "Do *you* wanna tell him?" He says, "No." I tell him, "Then forget about it. It's fine." Sinatra realizes I never said, "Cut." He winds up between two cameras and he gives me a look like "Was that okay?" I truly believe he would've done another take if I'd asked him, but I ask him, "You happy?" He says, "Yeah." I tell him, "Then I'm happy," and that's that. He's there less than three minutes for a twenty-second scene, but he's wonderful and the show turns out great. I only get to spend two minutes and forty-nine seconds with Frank Sinatra, but it's two minutes and forty-nine seconds more than most people ever get.

Between 1996 and 1997, I direct three episodes of *Everybody Loves Raymond*. I love working with the cast. I know Peter Boyle from our improv days and *Steelyard Blues*. I know Doris Roberts from working with her on *Angie* and *Rhoda*. I know Brad Garrett from a short-lived show I directed called *First Impressions* in 1988. And I like Ray Romano a lot. The show is something of a throwback to old-fashioned sitcoms such as *The Dick Van Dyke Show*, although Ray isn't the physical comedian that Dick is. You have a family, a kitchen, a living room, etc. instead of what they're doing on other shows with one camera and shooting exteriors. Comedies have gotten complicated, but *Raymond* is a return to the simplicity of one main set. If we have scenes that take place someplace else, we have what's called "a swing set" that can be dressed to resemble whatever other location is called for. But there's always a main set that the audience gets used to and with it, there's a level of comfort and I like that.

Working on *Everybody Loves Raymond* is not the great experience it might've been, not because of the cast or the premise, but because the Executive Producer, Phil Rosenthal, is another control freak who needs to be on top of every detail, like Danny Arnold on *Fish* and Paul Haggis on *City*. On one episode, I tell Phil, "Any note you give me I promise you I will give to the cast, but it should come from me as the director, so there's no confusion." Forget about it. He gives notes while I'm standing there like a jerk. He changes the blocking, whatever. It's an inability to give up power and delegate authority. It's his show and he needs to do it himself. I have a theory about all of these writers who become Executive Producers: Their attitude is that they're too busy to direct, so they have to hire some schmuck to do it. Otherwise, they would do it themselves and it would be perfect. Another problem is that you get a guy that's a wonderful writer, he creates a wonderful show, you make him an Executive Producer, and the contract gives him final cut. Well, if it's his first show, he's never been in an editing bay in his life. He's a writer, but he has the power.

On *Everybody Loves Raymond*, I show up in the editing room and I can sense they're annoyed that I'm there. In one scene, Peter Boyle is talking to Ray Romano about a haircut and they're using the master shot. I ask the editor, "Why don't you go to the single? I have a nice, tight closeup." You need to see his haircut, in order for the joke to work. The editor says, "Phil wants to use the master." There's nothing I can do, because Phil has final cut. Nowadays, TV directors have no control. They use a quad screen, so they're watching all four cameras on one little monitor, the director's standing there watching it, behind him is the Executive Producer and the Producer, behind them is the network, behind the network is the studio – and *every* one of them has an opinion about the shot. When I'm shooting *film*, they have no idea what they have until it's all edited together. Even when I'm shooting on tape, before the quad, you don't have that problem. Now, it's different.

On my first episode, Phil insists on shooting the rehearsal for the audience. What isn't taken into consideration is that the Technical Director is cutting the show as he goes, because I'm down on the set working with the actors, not up in the booth watching the monitor with everybody else. On the first day, I mark all my shots as we go along, then I go up and give them to the Technical Director – who sabotages me. I know what I want every step of the way, but the Technical Director wants to direct. I don't want a show shot by somebody else, even if it's only a rehearsal. That Technical Director goes on to direct the next couple of seasons of the show, because Phil has someone who will do whatever he wants without questioning any of it. Well, that's not me and it never was.

In 1996, Nickelodeon flies me to Orlando, Florida, to work on a new show called *Kenan & Kel*, starring Kenan Thompson and Kel Mitchell. The Producer who hires me, Brian Robbins, played one of the kids on *Head of the Class*. At one point, we both receive Best Children's Show Directors Guild nominations – Brian for *First Time* and me for an episode of *Kenan & Kel*. He beats me. I wind up directing four episodes. Doing a sitcom for teens isn't really any different than doing one for adults. The kids on that show work well together; they really find a nice combination of actors. Afterwards, Kenan becomes a regular on *Saturday Night Live*.

CHAPTER THIRTY-TWO

For more than twenty years, I have led an unusual and informal group of guys known as Yarmy's Army. Here's the story behind it all: I'm friends with a guy named Dick Yarmy, the actor-brother of *Get Smart* star, Don Adams. Dick is a lovely man who adores his wife, Alice, and adores his daughter, Claudia, but he is an inveterate gambler. Alice begs him to stop gambling countless times, but it never sticks and she ends up divorcing him. His gambling addiction is so bad, he has an arrangement whereby if the racetrack is open, his agent doesn't call him to go on auditions unless it's before or after the track is open.

In the early '90s, Dick is in Philadelphia, playing one of the guys in the poker game in *The Odd Couple*. He doesn't feel well, so he goes to a doctor, who diagnoses him with lung cancer. He calls up his friends, because he needs to vent. We tell him to get some funny videos and books to cheer him up and entertain him and he says, "Hey, schmucks! You're all funny! Why do I need to watch funny videos and read funny books? Take me to lunch and make me *laugh*!" Dick leaves *The Odd Couple* and returns to L.A. We have our first lunch at an Italian restaurant on Ventura Boulevard in Sherman Oaks. Present are Dick, producer Sam Denoff, Harvey Korman, Ronnie Schell, Chuck McCann, Hank Bradford – the head writer on *The Tonight Show* – and me. We have a great time laughing and telling stories, and nobody has a better time than Dick. We get the bill and we're trying to figure out what we should tip. Bradford asks, "Hey Dick, what do you tip your chemo guy?" Dick loves it. After three or four weekly lunches, we get thrown out for making too much noise, so we change to another place in Sherman Oaks and we shift to dinners instead of lunches. Dick comes to the dinners and laughs long and hard. One night, he starts coughing while I'm telling a story, so I say, "What are you *doing*? You're killing my *timing*! You want to cough, go outside! Don't use the cancer as an excuse! Go *outside* and cough!" Everybody starts chiming in, "Yeah, Dick! Get the fuck *outta* here!" It may sound mean and disrespectful, but he understands what we're doing and he loves it.

We have red caps made up – long before Donald Trump stole our idea – that say "YARMY'S ARMY" across the front, but we don't tell Dick about them. At one dinner, we have the caps on our laps and when he walks in, we all stand up and put them on our heads. Dick starts to cry. It's really a wonderful moment. Yarmy's Army starts to grow, eventually including such notables as Tom Poston, Howie Morris, Shelley Berman, Louis Nye, Don Knotts, Pat Harrington and Pat McCormick. Tim Conway, who worked with Dick in a few plays, also "enlists."

At one of our dinners, I have a run-in with a heavyset actor named Gailard Sartain. Our rule is, "You don't smoke in the room when we're eating, out of respect for Dick's lung cancer and as a courtesy to the rest of us." Well, in addition to being a smoker, Sartain is a drinker. He's a little loaded and he walks into the room with a lit cigarette. I tell him, "You can't smoke in here. We've all agreed to that. You'll have to smoke outside." He gives me an annoyed look and he stands in the doorway with the cigarette, staring daggers at me. Everybody settles in. Sartain's sitting there with his drink, but without his cigarette. He's watching me, and he's getting angrier and angrier. As we're leaving, he stops me in the hallway and he says, "You don't like me, do you?" I tell him, "I don't dislike you. I told you what our rules are. You can't smoke in the room with everybody there." He says, "Admit it. You don't like me." I tell him, "Look, this discussion is going nowhere," and I start to walk away. Sartain grabs my arm. I tell him, "Get your fuckin' hand off me." He steps back and says, "You want to take me on?" I tell him, "If there's anybody here that'll take you on, it's me." I'm thinking to myself, "He's a big fuckin' guy. If he falls on me, it's over. He'll break my ribs. Do I stick my fingers in his eye? Do I blind him? Do I hit him in the throat? I can't wrestle with him or he'll kill me. I've gotta take the first shot and make sure I hurt him." After all these years, I might just as well be back on Henry Street sticking up for my pals, or staring down Big Ralph at The Copa in Youngstown! By this time, everybody has gathered around and they get in the middle of it and stop it before it starts. All this over a lousy cigarette! Some months later, I'm in the hospital because I've had a heart attack. Sartain sends me a card saying, "It wasn't that big a deal. I don't know why you had a heart attack." I send him back a note that says, "If you're smart, you'll fight me *now*."

The members of Yarmy's Army work out a schedule so that every day Dick has to have radiation or chemo, there are up to three people available to go with him. That way, if one of us gets a call to go out on an audition or is out of town, there will still be someone to take Dick to the hospital for his treatments. Dick ends up missing only one dinner in the six or seven months we meet, because he doesn't feel up to it. In May of 1992, we get a call at about eleven in the morning that Dick has passed away. Everybody gathers at the hospital. There must be forty people in the hallway wanting to say goodbye. The nurses are in shock and tell us they've never seen anything like it. One by one, we kiss his cheek and say goodbye.

We have a memorial for Dick at Theatre West. After the service, nobody is moving to get into their car. We're standing out on the sidewalk talking to each other, hugging each other. We don't want it to end, so we decide to keep Yarmy's Army going – even though Dick is gone. We continue to meet, once a month, raising a glass in a toast to Dick's memory at each meeting. I come up with the idea of putting on some shows using our own talent, so we can get some money together and help actors who aren't as fortunate as we are. We start putting on Yarmy's Army benefit shows and on at least two occasions, we get upwards of $50,000. One is a salute to the U.S. Navy on their 200th anniversary and the other is New Year's Eve in Wisconsin. We give everybody a couple of thousand to cover their expenses and the rest goes into an account so that we can give it away. Our arrangement for the benefit shows is: No matter how big a name you are, no one gets top billing; it's always alphabetical. We do shows with Harvey and Tim and Shelley, and they all accept alphabetical order.

Every once in a while, Dick's brother, Don Adams, shows up and disrupts the whole thing. He comes to Yarmy's Army one day and announces, "I understand you're making all this money and *giving* it to people. I want an accounting of all that money. I want to know where all the money's going." I tell him, "Don, I bought a house on the island of Jamaica. *That's* where the money went." He shows up every three or four months just to complain about something: "Why are you going and doing these shows? I thought this was supposed to be about having dinner and just having some laughs." I tell him, "Don, what's wrong with helping other actors who are not as lucky as we are – in your *brother's* name?" He says, "If you're gonna continue doing this, I want you to take the name off. You can't use the name 'Yarmy.'" Everybody starts to laugh. I tell him, "Don, you gotta be kidding me! You haven't been 'Yarmy' for over sixty years! And one more point: 'Yarmy' is not 'Sinatra.' You don't get that kind of attention with it. I'll stop using the name 'Yarmy' when Claudia tells me to." Claudia is Dick's daughter. Don calls me a dictator, we go back and forth for a while, and he leaves. That's the last we see of Don Adams.

The restaurant in Sherman Oaks where we've been meeting goes out of business, so we move to Jerry's Deli in Westwood for a while. Jerry's keeps raising their prices, so we switch to the Shanghai Grill in Beverly Hills and that becomes our home until 2015, when we shift to Fu's Palace in West L.A., but wherever we take our movable feast, Yarmy's Army persists.

CHAPTER THIRTY-THREE

Somewhere along the line, my marriage to Anita goes sour, even though we manage to hang in for an impressive thirty-one years. Anita goes to school to study psychology, which I encourage. She's extremely bright, very good at what she does, and she becomes a psychotherapist. In the process, however, she becomes a workaholic. She goes to work at nine o'clock in the morning and isn't home till eight-thirty. Then she eats alone and reads the papers. It gets to the point where we're roommates instead of husband and wife, miles and miles apart.

When Casey and Anthony are about fourteen and sixteen, Anita and I separate with the intention of getting back together. It's a terrible time. I move out and have to rent a furnished apartment and I just hate it. The boys come and spend a night with me and then go back to the house. It's awful, so I move back in. It may be a cliché, but we hang in for the sake of the kids and we hope things will somehow change and get better, but they don't. It's all very depressing. Finally, I tell Anita, "This can't go on anymore. I'm becoming a bitter old man and I don't want that, so unless you're willing to make some changes, I'm out. And when I leave this time, I'm not coming back. This won't be another trial separation." I sit down to lunch with Anthony and Casey and I tell them, "I'm leaving, but I will still be there for you." I write them both letters telling them how much I love them and that I will always be there to support them in every way possible. Instead of being shocked by the news, they tell me, "We don't know how you stayed this long." Casey says, "I never saw any affection between the two of you. I remember seeing you hug Mom once and her arms were down by her side the whole time." I want to take a moment to thank Anita for the gift of these two *wonderful* young men.

I leave and take an apartment on Rexford with a year's lease. About a month after I'm out on my own, I call my friend, Patricia

Ridgely, and ask her to dinner. It's been about four or five years since her husband, actor-impressionist Bob Ridgely, died of cancer. There's already a friendship with Patricia and, frankly, I've been lonesome for years, even when I was married. I invite Patricia to dinner and that's it. We realize what a spark there is. Patricia and I marry in 2010 and it has been a *very* happy union. At our wedding, I get up and make the following toast: "I want to thank Patricia for bringing love and laughter back into my life and for lowering my blood pressure to 120 over 70. And when the little boy in me needs a place to hide, you are my secret treehouse."

In 2011, I take Patricia to New York for her birthday and we go to see *Relatively Speaking*, an evening of one-act plays. One play is by Ethan Coen, and directed by John Turturro. Another is written and directed by Elaine May. The last one, *Honeymoon Motel*, is written and directed by Woody Allen. It's hilarious, and as I look around, I realize I've directed *everybody* in the play at one time or another, including Julie Kavner, Mark-Linn Baker, Steve Guttenberg and Richard Libertini. I ask Julie, "Has Woody been in a lot?" She says, "He comes in once a week." I ask her, "To give notes?" She tells me, "No, he just says, 'I think I've got a better joke here.'"

In recent years, I've been devoting myself more to the "legitimate theatre" – both on and off the stage – rather than television and film. In 2004, Pat Harrington and I put on a show called *Harrington & Storm: Two Guys Doing A One-Man Show* at Garry Marshall's Falcon Theatre in Toluca Lake and later at Theatre West in Los Angeles. It's written by Pat, Michael Rhodes and myself. As an ending to the show, I suggest to Pat, "Wouldn't it be fun if you played your Irish guy and I played my Jewish guy?" Our characters meet on a park bench every day and hang out. He's a retired stevedore from Ireland and I'm a retired barber. I base it on Sam the Barber in the building where I grew up, who used to send me out for loose cigarettes.

The show runs its course and I realize there's a whole play in those two characters, so we develop that short sketch into a full-blown play called *Jimmy & Sam*. Pat has difficulty learning all the lines for such a sizable and demanding role. The director and I dread the idea of having to call Pat the next morning and tell him we have to replace him. But that night, my phone rings: It's Pat, who tells me he'd spoken with his wife, Sally, and he can't do the play. Although we couldn't have known it at the time, these were the early signs of the Alzheimer's that would eventually take the life of my dear friend in 2016. Pat's replaced by a wonderful actor named Clem Blake and, in 2011, we open at Theatre 40 in Beverly Hills. At the end of the play, my character isn't feeling well, so he takes out a bottle of Tums and as he goes to open it, he drops the bottle, grabs his chest, has a heart attack, and dies right onstage. One night, I hear a woman in the first row say, "Oy, just what we need – for people our age to watch a man *die!*" Each night, as people are leaving, we hear them discussing the ending: "Why'd he die?" "He shouldn't have died!" "I think it's okay that he dies," and so on. The play is well-received. Sadly, six weeks after the shows closes, Clem Blake dies of complications from Hepatitis C.

The following year, I star in a play called *The Last Romance*. My character, Ralph, is an 80-year-old widower. Even though I'm 81 at the time, the director, James Paradise, thinks I don't look old enough, so I grow a gray-white beard to give a stronger sense of my advanced years. That part is a real challenge, because I'm onstage for the entire show and there's a lot to memorize. It actually costs me money to do that play, because I spend hundreds of dollars on a hypnotist to help me deal with such a demanding role. It's worth it. She tells me, "Just remember: You are Ralph, so anything you say onstage is fine. Don't worry about the lines; just say whatever feels right." That puts me at ease and I'm able to do the play.

In 2014, I direct *The Love List* at Theatre 40 with John Combs, Martin Thompson and Jennifer Laks. The three of them are so inventive, I have precious little "directing" to do. I give them a note here and a suggestion there, but that's it. At one point, John is talking about knowing that Jennifer – his dream girl – is not real. He says, "I don't want to give it up. She kisses me. She *likes* kissing me," and he almost cries. It's a reference to his ex-wife, who didn't like kissing him, so he starts to tear up. That's not direction; that's his choice, and I think, "Wow. That's beautiful!" If you're a director who has to be hands-on all the time, you can *kill* a moment like that.

The following year, I have the pleasure of directing my old friend Dick Cavett in *Hellman v. McCarthy* at Theatre 40. It's all about the contentious relationship between writers Lillian Hellman and Mary McCarthy and it centers on their *Dick Cavett Show* appearances. Flora Plumb plays Lillian Hellman. At first, we have the set for Cavett's interview on stage left, the center is a table for meetings with the lawyers, and on stage right is Lillian Hellman's kitchen. I think to myself, "The center of this play is really Cavett and the interview," so I move their chairs center stage. Flora comes in that afternoon and she's completely thrown by the change in the setup. She asks, "Why don't you just put my kitchen in the *audience*?!" A half-hour later, she says, "I have to apologize. I freaked when I saw the set." I tell her, "It's okay. If you weren't such a good actress, I'd tell you to go fuck yourself." Flora is marvelous. You actually *watch* her grow old onstage. It just knocks me out. The whole cast is so good that I hardly give any notes. When you've got something bubbling like that, you don't stop it; you just let it go.

When you're directing three or four actors, each one might have a different approach. One may be heavy-duty Method, another just reacts and plays off whatever's going on. As a director, it's my responsibility to understand that, so the guy who's the Method actor isn't getting in the way of the actor who just comes in and does it. Jimmy Cagney's advice about acting is, "Learn your lines, plant your feet, look the other actor in the eye, say the words, and *mean* them." Brilliant. That's really what it's about: You look the other actor in the eye, you listen to what he's saying, and then you answer *honestly*, even though the words are not your own.

EPILOGUE

When I started out in show business, my ultimate dream was to make a thousand dollars a week. I never dreamed I would have the career that I had. I'm very fortunate to have worked with so many wonderful stars, from Frank Sinatra to Robin Williams to Billy Crystal to Woody Allen, and so many more.

To reach my age and still have friends that I have known for sixty or seventy years is truly amazing. Sadly, I have also lost a lot of dear friends along the way. I'm enjoying my "golden years." In fact, they are the best years of my life (thank you, Patricia). I no longer direct television, but I work in theater, which is my first love. I also play a lot of tennis and, believe it or not, I can still run down many shots. To sum it all up: I am a very happy, healthy, and lucky man.

ABOUT THE AUTHORS

Howard Storm is an actor, standup comic, improv teacher, and prolific television director who grew up on the mean streets of New York's Lower East Side during the Great Depression. After playing rough-and-tumble, mob-owned clubs in the '50s and graduating to big-time nightclubs in the '60s, Howard directed numerous episodes of such classic TV series as *Rhoda, Laverne & Shirley, Mork & Mindy, Taxi* and *Everybody Loves Raymond*, as well as the feature film *Once Bitten*. He lives in Beverly Hills with his wife, Patricia.

Steve Stoliar is a screenwriter, producer, and voice actor who has written for such television series as *Murder She Wrote, Simon & Simon, The New WKRP in Cincinnati*, and *Sliders*, as well as producing documentaries on such varied subjects as The Marx Brothers, John Lennon, and Dr. Martin Luther King, Jr. Steve also penned a memoir, *RAISED EYEBROWS: My Years Inside Groucho's House*, which is in development as a motion picture. He lives in Studio City with his cat, Oskar.

Howard Storm and Steve Stoliar

INDEX

Made in the USA
Middletown, DE
21 January 2020